Transforming Emotion

For my mother Sheila Fredman
from whom I continue to learn new ways of transforming
meaning and experience

Transforming Emotion

Conversations in counselling and psychotherapy

by

G LENDA F REDMAN

W
WHURR PUBLISHERS
LONDON AND PHILADELPHIA

© 2004 Whurr Publishers Ltd
First published 2004
by Whurr Publishers Ltd
19b Compton Terrace
London N1 2UN England and
325 Chestnut Street, Philadelphia PA 19106 USA

British Library Cataloguing in Publication Data

A catalogue record for this book
is available from the British Library.

ISBN 1 86156 399 X

Typeset by Adrian McLaughlin, a@microguides.net

Contents

Acknowledgements

The day after I signed the contract for this book, I broke my left (writing) hand. Colin Whurr's generous response to the news that I would have to delay submitting the manuscript helped me to get going again when I was able. Many thanks also go to Alessandra Lemma who introduced me to Whurr Publishers Ltd and to my colleagues and friends who refrained from interpreting my experience! The ideas I present in the pages that follow have been formed and shaped over decades, in conversations with many different people. My utmost appreciation goes to all the clients, trainees, supervisees, course participants, tutors, supervisors and my family and friends with whom I have created the material that follows. In particular I am indebted to the people who have given me permission to print exerpts of our conversations – there is no way I could have found better words than theirs to speak the theories I share in this book.

Many colleagues have generously shared with me their time, their references and their stories. In particular I am grateful to those working within the Camden and Islington Learning Disability Service and the Camden and Islington Older People's Psychology Team. Deborah Christie and Angela Griffin helped me extend my repertoire of approaches to 'emotional presupposing'. We have been privileged to have the creative contributions of Henrik Lynggaard, Alison Milton, Dimitri Sklavounos, Peter Pearce, Alison Pearce, Sally Donati, Elan Hoffman, Andia Papadopoulou, Eleni Yerolaki and Tresa Andrews who have joined our systemic paediatric psychology team at the Middlesex Hospital over the years.

Adam Phillips's personal sharing of the frustrations and joys of writing encouraged me to persevere at times when I feared that I was losing the plot. Peter Lang's supervision continues to inspire me with the confidence to extend my abilities in therapeutic conversations. His words have enabled me to transform my experiences in many facets of my life. Philip Messent, my partner, has always willingly read drafts of each chapter. His ability to make challenging critique palatable in many creative ways has made completion of this book possible. Without his loving presence on what at times has felt like an emotional roller-coaster, this book would never have been written.

Foreword

ADAM PHILLIPS

The title of this remarkable book, *Transforming Emotion*, in its apparently simple and understated ambiguity, introduces us to the idea that our emotions are always a work in progress, never finished, never formulated once and for all. We transform our emotions, more often than we perhaps notice, through conversation (how we were feeling and what we supposedly felt was what our very first conversations were about). And our emotions transform us, transform our sense of ourselves and what we are like, as we change from mood to mood. What we call our feelings, Fredman suggests, might be more like snatches of conversation in search of more conversation, rather than the sound-bites of self-knowledge we take them to be. Our feelings are not already there, just needing to be expressed, like a collection of objects that can be put on show; they are more like experiments in collaboration, forms of participation, ways of joining in. We should not, in other words, go on hiding behind the idea that we are trying to express ourselves. Indeed that idea itself may be part of the problem. In what Fredman calls our 'emotion talk', as she makes startlingly clear, we are doing something far more interesting than that.

'I approach emotions,' Fredman writes in her Introduction – and it is integral to her style as both clinician and writer to approach rather than merely confront or define or take over – 'as activities, abilities, relationships and performances rather than as expressions of what is inside. Thus I look at expressing emotions as ways of "being with" each other.' Our emotions are not so much evidence of our solitude, as our ways of being together. Our emotions are what we do with each other. In a therapy culture bewitched by simple oppositions, inside/outside, love/hate, doctor/patient, we are forced to make spurious choices; we have to locate who we are and where we are and what we feel too narrow-mindedly. *Transforming Emotion* reveals, without needing to expose or accuse anyone, just how coercive and limiting these options are; and the kind of world they constitute. A world, for example, in which experts can tell us – or 'help us to see' – what is inside us and what is outside, what is really love and what is really hate, and so on. In Fredman's approach, which is at once utterly practical and undiminishing of the poetry of feeling, the only expertise available is conversational.

Despite their best intentions, or because of them, most therapies tend to be more or less subtle ways of stopping the conversation. As the fascinating and poignant therapeutic conversations in this book show – and it is integral to the spirit of Fredman's book that it is conversations that are quoted, and not theoretical pronouncements – 'emotion as a communication or invitation to others to respond' is quite different from the conventional idea of emotion as 'experienced feelings' (p. 103). It is the difference between emotion as unfinished business – an invitation needs a response in order to work, in order to be an invitation – and emotion as something pre-packaged. Emotion only makes sense as what Fredman calls, 'continually forming emotion' (p. 118); and, 'since feelings are often experienced as ambiguous or mixed rather than pure, multiple descriptions of emotion are usually possible' (p. 110). What this means in practice is that definitive formulation about how we are feeling – the attempt to find a final description, or indeed the assumption that there is a core set of emotions that we already know of – is a way of distracting us from our emotional life. What we thought was therapeutic may be just pre-emptive; what we thought of as self-expression was fear of the future. In short, Fredman's plainly eloquent, undogmatic proposals make much of our theorizing about therapy both redundant and misleading. Read in the spirit in which it is written – with the kind of curiosity that does not need to take refuge in inner superiority (or blaming, which is the same thing) – Transforming Emotion makes one wonder what the future of therapy writing, of therapy talk might be. After all, if therapists and theorists stop telling us the truth about ourselves what are they going to tell us? Fredman wants us to keep faith with the unknown; and her word for this faith is conversation.

In the conclusion to her previous book, Death Talk, Fredman (1997) left us with a misgiving about maps, about what we use to know where we are and where we are going. 'Although I was enjoying the sense of security and direction my emergent map was giving me,' she wrote (p. 124), 'over time I began to recognize that I tended to follow the map at the expense of my relationship with my clients. I noticed how I was missing information they were giving me and losing connection with them, as my close attention to this map distracted me from attending to their feelings or following their communications that did not fit with or confirm it.'

Maps, as Fredman intimates, are so much smaller than the ground they seem to cover. In Transforming Emotion, which is so many things at once – a radical critique of the therapy culture and a new picture of collaboration, of how people might speak to each other without intimidation: an extraordinary redescription of what it might be to help someone, and of what it might be to write about helping someone; a meditation on maps – Fredman has given us an undistracting map. By not making claims for itself this subtle and inspiring book has reclaimed conversation for us. It has been surprisingly difficult for the talking therapies to do justice to the real resonance of conversation. After reading Fredman's book one's listening will never be the same again.

Being with people in emotion

About eight years ago I was privileged to join Peter Lang and Zethu Makathini in training community workers in South Africa. We were asked to focus on counselling people affected by violence. Many of the participants attending our courses had themselves been affected by severe violent attacks on their communities, families, properties or their own person. During a training exercise in which participants were practising interviewing each other in small groups of four, one of the community workers began to weep as she shared a distressing personal story with her colleagues. In response, the woman interviewing her stopped talking and began to hum quietly and gently with the rhythm of her weeping. Gradually the other two women in their group joined in, humming and harmonizing with each other and with the weeping of their colleague. In time sweet sounds filled the training room as other course participants contributed their voices to the harmony. An immense feeling of warmth touched me in this moment. I was moved from concern for the weeping woman to a desire to join the harmonies and rhythms that she was creating with her colleagues.

Since that time I have wanted to find ways to *be with* clients in emotion that capture how those women were with their colleague as she wept. The interviewer and her co-participants acknowledged and respected the weeping woman's voice. Joining with her rhythm, they co-ordinated with her crying. In this way the weeping woman was included rather than isolated from everyone witnessing her expression of emotion. Thus the others connected with her experience rather than expected her to attend to their expert opinion of her needs. Everyone involved and concerned was able to participate in a rewarding interaction towards collaboratively creating a sense of community. At no time did they instruct or constrain her from her personal expression. By joining, co-ordinating and collaborating they seemed able to transform her solitary distress into a joint achievement of harmony.

This episode has stayed with me over the years and has shaped the approach to transforming emotion that I present in this book. In the chapters that follow, therefore, I propose practices intended to support the sorts of experiences of co-ordination, belonging and self-worth that I witnessed the women above making possible. Those women inspired me to find a way of working with people in emotion that invites and enables the voices of everyone involved to be heard rather than one that silences or marginalizes voices, colonizes language and so disempowers people. I wanted to find ways of collaborating with and including the persons expressing emotion, as those community workers did with their weeping colleague, rather than isolating or dividing them from those intending to help. These intentions guide the practices that I present in this book.

I work as a clinical psychologist and systemic psychotherapist with people referred to psychology departments within the public health service. I also supervise, consult and train qualified practitioners (clinical psychologists, counsellors, social workers, psychotherapists, doctors, nurses, physiotherapists, and occupational and speech therapists) in their work with patients and clients presenting with a range of problems. One of the most common issues practitioners bring to supervision relates to feelings and emotions of self and others, for example, 'How do I talk with this person about his feelings?', 'She is asking for help with how to feel', 'How do I manage my own feelings about this?', 'How should I respond?'. Many practitioners have shared their disillusion with the verbal therapies that involve naming, interpreting or encouraging the expression of feelings which, although sometimes providing insight and even illumination, they have found often leave people unmoved and therefore unchanged. Many practitioners I have met have also found their thinking and relationships with clients constrained by an impoverished language of emotion, which has sometimes invited their clients' refusal, hostility or withdrawal. These practitioners have usually been taking what I refer to as an 'autonomous' approach to emotion.

In Chapter 1, I reflect on how different discourses inform how we act and interact with others in emotion. I distinguish 'autonomous' and 'relational' emotion discourses illustrating how each 'world view' tells a different story about the nature, location, function, meaning and development of emotion and therefore informs the language, rules, words and bodily expressions we use to speak about and perform emotion. For example, an autonomous discourse locates emotions within the individual and therefore views emotion as innate, universal, subjective, personal and essentially bodily. Autonomous emotion practices would therefore most likely focus on the sensation and distinction of the emotion like the naming, interpreting and encouraging expression of emotion mentioned above. A relational discourse on the other hand approaches emotion as created between people and therefore communal and connected with cultural logic. Relational emotion practices would therefore focus on co-ordinating with others and on how emotion stories are created in the contexts of relationships and cultures.

This book will invite you, the reader, into a relational approach to emotions. Within this perspective, I also incorporate the physical experience of emotions, yet go beyond sensation to approach emotion as a narrative, which incorporates stories about the body in the context of relationships and meanings. I also address the performing of emotions in the context of this matrix of relationships and meanings. Hence I approach emotions as constructed in relationship and context and in the 'doing' of the feeling between people.

Throughout this book I acknowledge that there is no universal story of emotion necessarily acceptable or familiar to all cultures. I also do not propose that one emotion 'world view' is superior to another. However I am clear that I am not taking a position of moral relativism whereby all perspectives are seen as equally desirable. Since each emotion discourse shapes our experience and thereby enables and constrains what we feel, think and do, I acknowledge that I might differentially affect people's sense of belonging and self-worth if I privilege one discourse over another while engaging with them in emotion. Therefore I propose that we evaluate, reflect on and take responsibility for the consequences of adopting different emotion practices for our selves, for others and for our relationships.

A good enough fit between people's emotion discourses is likely to enable a comfortable co-ordination and coherence in how they relate with each other in emotion. On the other hand, when emotion discourses are contradictory, we are less likely to understand each other's emotion language or create shared meanings with each other and are more likely to experience each other's communications as an affront, oppressive or constraining. In Chapter 1, therefore, I show how, in therapeutic conversations, we might begin to explore the emotion discourses people privilege, paying careful attention to the language, rules and theories of all people in the conversation so as to enable more co-ordinated than colonizing emotion talk. Hence I discuss how, in a therapeutic conversation, we might join the emotion discourse of people with whom we are talking, work towards co-creating new, shared language and rules and possibly transform emotions through our emotion talk.

Assuming the authority to distinguish and name feelings on behalf of others implies that people have not only different abilities, but also different rights and responsibilities for naming feelings. In Chapter 2, therefore, I discuss how the naming of emotions is a powerful act that can risk coercion, undermining the other person, colonizing his or her language or creating an impasse in communication if not satisfactorily negotiated. In my attempts to avoid coercion, colonizing or undermining people, therefore, I always try to participate in the creation of words that describe their experience in ways that resonate and fit best for them rather than imposing my preferred vocabulary of emotion. I propose, therefore, paying careful attention to the language and meanings people are using in the moment towards creating a shared language and understanding of emotions. Since we cannot start from the position that we all share a common language of emotion that accurately transfers meanings and experience between people, I propose that we approach the meaning of words as uniquely related to the people we are talking with. Therefore, I offer relational practices towards creating a shared language and common understanding of emotion which involve joining the language of the other, adopting an attitude of curiosity and exploring emotions through the contexts of people's lives.

I approach emotion as the story we weave of our sensation, display and judgements through the multi-layered contexts of our lives. We create emotion stories in relationships with others, for example family, community and colleagues, and therefore with reference to the memories and stories of our cultures. To know how to go on with people in emotion, requires an understanding of the contexts of their emotion – what judgements they make, what stories inform those judgements and what rules guide their actions. In Chapter 3, therefore, I describe how we might explore, with curiosity, the moral orders of people's emotion through the different contexts of their lives, listening for the judgements they are making about expression of their feeling and the rules informing their display. I propose that transforming emotion involves changing the storyline. Exploring people's stories and judgements through the contexts of their lives creates possibilities for loosening unhelpful or constraining emotion stories thus opening space for alternative stories that might invite positive views of self and relationships. I go on to present ways in which we might invite or introduce alternative emotion stories.

In Chapter 3, I also discuss how emotion stories are intricately woven with our stories of identity and therefore have implications for how we perceive the moral worth of ourselves. I share conversations with clients who have taught me to be mindful of the sorts of descriptions of emotions that create negative stories of identity and point out that my autonomous naming of emotions on behalf of the other alone has rarely enhanced our communication. I note that emotion names are most commonly refused when the name connects to a story that undermines a person's sense of worthiness or autonomy or suggests incompetence. I reflect here on how we might co-create stories that enhance rather than diminish people's identities.

Since we live within our bodies, communicating feelings to each other and understanding each other's feelings always involves the body. In Chapter 4, I introduce the body into our developing story of emotion, taking a relational perspective of the body as communicator of feelings rather than an autonomous perspective of the body as container of feelings. Since stories hold our emotions together, co-ordinating our bodies with our judgements and actions and exploring bodily experiences can offer another way into stories of emotion. I introduce approaches to transforming emotion stories that begin with bodily feelings and postures, for example resonating with and mirroring the body posture of the other, connecting the body with emotion stories and finding the story connected with the preferred posture.

In the first four chapters, I discuss how our beliefs, the stories we tell and the discourses that inform them, position us morally, bodily and hence relationally with one another. In Chapter 5, I go on to address how professionals might prepare for conversations with clients by reflecting on the emotional postures ('emotional presupposing') they might expect to meet and might themselves carry into the therapeutic relationship. I suggest relational practices to enable practitioners to transform unwanted emotional postures towards positions that are more likely to invite an atmosphere of respect, safety and collaboration for the people involved. These include changing emotional postures through using our beliefs about emotion as resources, reflecting on multiple perspectives and deconstructing the practitioner's emotion discourses.

If the South African woman above had analysed, interpreted or attempted to name her colleague's feeling as she wept, she would have involved herself in a 'rational' sort of understanding in which she might have tried to step out of the process before she acted. Instead she responded to her colleague's responses with her body and thus was engaged in a 'responsive' and 'relational' sort of understanding that I reflect on in Chapter 4. In Chapter 6, I point out how assuming that we 'know already' what is the best way to respond to the other's feeling disconnects us from the people involved as we become more involved in our relationships with what we know than with the people we are intending to help. Intending to 'know from' the other, on the other hand, positions us to connect with them in joint activity. In Chapter 6, I approach emotions as activities, abilities, relationships and performances rather than as expressions of what is inside. Thus I look at expressing emotions as ways of 'being with' each other. I work towards creating contexts in which we can all participate in more rewarding interactions thereby diminishing a sense of isolation just as the women above performed with their colleague. My intention is to enable movement from a relationship pattern in which the individual showing emotion is isolated or alienated by shifting the focus from an individual problem to a joint achievement. This involves making opportunities for all to participate in the interaction by attending not only to the individual but also to the relationships. Therefore I describe how I position the person expressing the emotion as the knower who is able to act, choose and direct and how I create spaces and opportunities for people to connect and collaborate with each other in a way that they might all pool their abilities.

In each chapter, I have challenged aspects of autonomous emotion discourses reflecting on the implications of performing those discourses for people's sense of self-worth and for their relationships. Each chapter also offers examples of relational practices informed by the relational world view presented as a counterpoint to the autonomous perspective. In Chapter 7, I review the autonomous and relational practices presented throughout the book. I also present further relational practices connecting them with the discourses that inform them. For example, I describe the practices involved in externalizing emotions which offer a useful antidote to the allure of internalizing emotion conversations that locate feelings inside the person and are likely to invite negative stories of identity.

I met the people presented in this book on hospital wards, in outpatient hospital clinics or at local therapy or counselling centres. In some circumstances I was able to videotape or audio-record sessions, with the consent of all those directly participating. I worked on my own with some people; with others I was joined by colleagues or trainees who assisted me as team members and note-takers during the session. Sometimes I recorded dialogue from memory immediately after the session and at times would ask people in the session if I might write down a particular phrase, expression, word or idea. For the sake of clarity I have lightly edited the dialogue presented here. I have also in the process removed some of my own repetitions, mutterings, hesitations and false starts, so my communications might come across as far more fluent, articulate and well-thought-out than occurred in the actual situations.

Throughout this book I use a practical theory intending my presentation of personal stories, transcripts of conversations and case vignettes, wherever possible to 'speak' the theory. I have chosen to distinguish these stories and transcripts from my theorizing within the text. The use of smaller print makes this possible but in no way is intended to foreground my words over those of others nor to diminish their stories or experience.

In order to ensure that the people presented cannot be recognized by others, I have changed their names and other potentially identifying characteristics. In some situations I have merged families or combined the experiences or reports of different people to construct one composite 'profile'. This approach is intended to protect anonymity further. For the reader who wants to follow a composite profile through the book, the appendix contains the 'names' and the corresponding chapters in the text, together with a brief summary of the person's background and circumstances.

Although this book shows my name as sole author, it is inspired and informed by several conversations I have joined or witnessed and many books I have read. It is also shaped by the feedback I have received from clients in the course of therapeutic conversations and from trainees, qualified practitioners and colleagues in supervision and training sessions. In this sense this book reflects multiple voices. I draw from the works of communication theorists, Vernon Cronen (Cronen, Johnson, and Lannaman, 1982) and Barnett Pearce (1989) and systemic therapists Gianfranco Cecchin (1987), Tom Andersen (1992; 1995), Peter Lang (Cronen and Lang, 1994), Harlene Anderson (1997) and Harold Goolishian (Anderson and Goolishian, 1992). I draw extensively from the social constructionist theories of Ken Gergen (1999) and Sheila McNamee (McNamee and Gergen, 1999), John Shotter (1993) and Rom Harré (Harré and Parrott, 1996; Davies and Harré, 1990) and the work of narrative therapists Michael White (1989; 1992), David Epston (1993), and James Griffith and Melissa Elliot Griffith (1996). Recently I have drawn considerable inspiration from Lois Holzman (1999) and Fred Newman's (Newman and Holzman, 1993) performance of Vygotzky's ideas. I apologize in advance should my use or application of any of these people's work or the attributions of any of my ideas to their original thinking or practice seem inappropriate or incongruous. However, I also anticipate that those authors will recognize that this book is written within the spirit of postmodern thinking, which acknowledges that our interpretations are influenced by the contexts from which and into which we act, thereby generating the potential for a multiplicity of perspectives.

Within a framework informed by communication theories, social constructionism, and systemic and narrative therapies therefore, I attempt to incorporate a range of research findings and theories of emotion, not as truths but as possibilities to guide conversations and actions with people in therapy. Thus in the pages that follow I intend to offer you, the reader, a repertoire of possibilities to talk about feelings and with feeling, to explore feelings with people, to make sense of feelings, to create and develop feelings, to use feelings and to co-ordinate feelings in relationships.

Throughout this book, I take the position there is no one correct way to think about emotions and hence treat all ideas as stories or theories that are neither right nor wrong but more or less useful. In this respect I am influenced by the systemic approach as described by Boscolo, Cecchin,

Hoffman and Penn (1987). Taking a 'not knowing position' (Anderson and Goolishian, 1992) in relation to people's beliefs and actions is intended to enable the systemic practitioner to adopt a non-evaluative stance and hence remain curious (Cecchin, 1987) about and connected with the client's meanings and stories. Rather than giving advice or interpretations informed by their own preferred theories or beliefs, systemic practitioners intend to ask questions that closely follow clients' feedback in an attempt to explore clients' preferred theses and explanations and thereby generate multiple views.

Informed by this ethos, I never assume that people meeting with me want to or even expect to talk about emotions. I remain mindful that a person can have good reasons not to engage in emotion talk, which may be experienced as threatening or undermining or may contravene their cultural moral order. I therefore rarely initiate a focus on emotion talk. Most usually I take my cue from the people I am engaging with. Often, emotion talk will arise naturally in our conversation. If clients initiate or invite me into emotion talk I follow. If someone else, like a referring professional or family member, has suggested that we talk about feelings, I always begin by addressing the contexts for talking. For example, I consider whether I am the person they prefer to talk with about feelings, or whether they have other members of their family, cultural or religious community or people of the same or different gender or sexuality they might prefer or want to include. To explore this I ask questions like, 'Whose idea was it that we meet and talk together?', 'What do you think of their suggestion that we talk about [sadness]?', 'Is there anyone else you would prefer to talk with/like to include?'. I also reflect on whether this is a suitable time or place for talking and take into account whether we have sufficiently created the sort of relationship which can enable a conversation about feelings in the way the client wants to have it, if at all. Thus I ask questions like, 'What are your views on our talking here together?', 'Are there some things you do not want to talk about here/with me?', 'How will I know if we are starting to talk in ways you do/do not want?'.

Hence I always begin with 'talking about emotion talk'. In this way I begin to create a context for talking with the clients which includes our exploring together whether and when it might be good or not to engage in emotion talk and the possible effects of talking about feelings on people and relationships (Fredman, 1997). I try to listen and respond from a posture of respectful curiosity, which invites mutual exploration about the clients' preferences.

The use of relationship questions, rather than statements or suggestions, is central to the systemic method (Tomm, 1988). I therefore ask questions about relationships between people and between versions of one's self. I also ask questions about the difference between people's views and between contexts. News of difference is intended to introduce new information (Bateson, 1979) to the interviewee and thereby create opportunities for new meanings to emerge and for possibilities of change. The choice of language and the juxtaposition of certain questions also introduce new information into our conversations and enable clients and me to make new connections. It is intended that clients become observers of their own thinking, actions and contexts in the process of considering their answers to systemic questions. My questions that address the effects or consequences of beliefs on actions or relationships, or of relationships on actions or beliefs, invited the people in this book to look at themselves and their situations from different perspectives.

In the course of this book I address emotions from different positions including those of professionals and clients. I also take different personal positions in relationship to the material. Therefore at times I speak with my voices of family and culture in relation to emotional experience. At other times I narrate with my professional voices in roles as helper, trainer, supervisor or consultant. I therefore move between references to 'clients', 'carers', 'professionals', 'people', 'patients', 'colleagues', and 'participants' in an attempt to reflect the relationship that has emerged in the course of a particular episode of communication. You, the reader, may choose to take different positions during your reading of this book. For example, you may elect to read from the perspective of a family member expressing emotions, a colleague affected by the emotions of another or a carer of someone who is showing emotion. You may also choose to read from the position of a person offering training or receiving supervision.

This book is therefore intended for people who work with emotions as well as for those whose interests lie in exploring their own understanding of emotions or extending their repertoire of abilities to talk about or be with others in emotion. Thus the approaches described can be used by helpers with clients, colleagues with each other, professionals in training or supervision who are required to make sense of, talk about and manage their own feelings and those of their patients and clients in the course of their routine work. It is also intended to be accessible to a general readership interested in exploring their own understanding of feelings and emotions and who want to develop their abilities to talk about feelings and perform emotions in different contexts. Since I take a systemic and social constructionist approach to feelings and emotions including an embodied 'doing' of emotions in the context of a relational matrix of cultural meanings, this book should have a multicultural application.

I present the ideas and practices that follow as offerings and invitations to you. It is not my intention to put forward here a picture of how things are, or a recipe for how they should be done. Therefore I will not be providing an inventory of emotions with corresponding theories and techniques designed to talk about feelings and manage emotion. (The most recent count I have come across is 412 emotions, many of which are identifiable only by women (Baron-Cohen, 2003).) Instead I will present a range of emotion theories and stories intended to offer openings to conversations and performances. I anticipate that you will be further elaborating the practices presented here as you use them creatively in your different contexts.

CHAPTER 1

Emotion talk

What are you feeling now?

> What feeling do you have now as you are reading these words?
>
> Describe the feeling. Where or how do you experience it? How does it affect you?
>
> I invite you, the reader, to reflect on these questions. Perhaps you would like to make some notes as you continue.
>
> If we were together now while you are reading this, how would I know you are feeling this way? What would I notice? Who, if they were present, would be most likely to notice you are feeling this way?
>
> If I, or someone else, were with you, what would you want us to notice about this feeling? What would you like us to do with the feeling?
>
> How do you know you are feeling what you describe?
>
> Is it positive or negative, or something else, to feel this way?
>
> Where do you get your ideas about this emotion from?

When Rita reflected on these questions at the start of a workshop I was running, she reported she 'felt bored', that the feeling was 'inside my head' and she experienced 'a fuzzy sort of blankness' so she felt 'a bit distracted'. She was not sure anyone else would notice or be affected by her feeling since it was 'inside' her but believed that if anyone did notice they 'would see the boredom' on her face. Rita said she would like 'someone to take the feeling away … maybe talking about this will get me out of it – get it out of my system'. She could not make sense of the question, 'How do you know you are feeling what you describe?' and responded, 'I don't know what you mean – everyone knows, I feel it in my body – you simply know, that kind of feeling we have when we are bored.'

Desmond, another course participant, reported he did not have any feelings to describe or discuss at the start of the workshop. 'I don't have a feeling. I'm OK … I've come here to learn something …' Desmond

11

agreed to be interviewed about his responses to these questions so we might extend our learning together. He explained that the rest of us participating with him on the workshop could not know what he was feeling since 'you don't know me so you can't know how I feel'. He said that some members of his family and some of his friends might know how he feels 'because they know where I'm coming from' but that he would not expect to discuss his feelings at work. I was particularly curious about Desmond's idea that you don't discuss your feelings at work and asked where that idea came from. Desmond explained that feelings 'interfere with focusing on the task in hand'; he was a charge nurse on a busy medical ward where nurses were encouraged to put their feelings aside and get on with the job. He recounted how impressed he had been with his nurse tutor's demonstration when she mimed how a good nurse takes off the feelings from home and hangs them on the hook with the coats at the start of each shift. At the end of our conversation, Desmond reflected that he had been very interested in our conversation and 'yes, this is making me think and I'm learning but I'm not sure yet what about …' and went on to say I had 'shaped' his emotion with the questions I asked – 'I didn't feel interested before … I do now … if you hadn't asked these questions, I wouldn't have felt anything'.

Rita, a white Irish social worker in her 40s, and Desmond, a younger black African nurse, responded to the same questions about their feelings in quite different ways. Their responses were probably informed by different discourses of emotion each representing diverse perspectives on emotions with different implications for how to act.

Emotion discourses

Within our cultures we participate in different discourses of emotion. A discourse comprises ideas and practices, beliefs, metaphors and rules that share common values and both reflects and constructs a specific world view (Burr, 1995). Therefore our discourses shape our experiences, enabling and constraining what we feel, think and do. Emotion discourses could include ideas about the nature of emotions and where they are located. For example, emotions are construed as irrational animal instincts, feminine weaknesses, driving forces, physiological impulses, diseases of the mind or ways of being and have been located inside the body, in behaviour, between people or within the spirits. Different discourses might also explain how emotions are generated, for example, they well up from within the person, are created between people or originate outside the person in food, the activities of other people, gods or spirits. Different powers are also attributed to emotion, as in they dominate and control, enliven, or affect balance. Each discourse therefore tells a different story about emotion and informs the language, rules, words and bodily expressions we use in our emotion talk to speak about emotion and with feeling. We might say, 'He barked at me', 'He was driven by fear', 'I am heartbroken' or 'She was blind with rage' and, depending on the story informing our talk, we might believe we should enhance or diminish emotions, express or control them. Hence different discourses of emotion inform how we experience our feelings, what feelings we attend to, what meanings we give to our feelings and how we act and interact with others in emotion. The emotion language, values and rules therefore inform the questions we ask about our own feelings and those of others and the meanings we go on to co-construct in emotion talk.

We might say that Rita was informed by an *autonomous* discourse of emotion since she experienced her feelings as subjective, personal and an expression of something inside of her. She was focusing on the sensation of her emotion and made a distinction between her mind and body, believing that her feeling was inside her body and could be managed if she were helped to ventilate it or get in touch with it. Consistent with an autonomous discourse, which construes emotions as innate and universal, Rita reports that one 'simply knows' the feeling of boredom since 'everyone knows' when they are bored.

Rita easily identified an internal bodily location for the feeling, 'inside me', and demonstrated a wide vocabulary for the sensations of her emotion including 'fuzzy', 'blankness', 'distracted'. Desmond, on the other hand, focused more on the contexts of his interpersonal relationships than on sensations or internal experiences. His comment that we were 'shaping' his emotion in the course of our conversation suggests he experienced his 'interest' as created between people and reflects a relational discourse of emotion. Desmond showed how he learnt the emotion rules of his nursing culture which obligates a good nurse to 'put your feelings aside and get on with the job' whereas Rita's autonomous discourse permits or perhaps even obligates her to talk about the feeling, as she says, to 'get it out of my system'.

Table 1.1 compares autonomous and relational discourses of emotion. Each discourse reflects and constructs our different views on emotion which both enable and constrain what we think, feel and do and thereby constitute our experience of emotion. Intimately connected to our cultures, these 'world views' have different implications for how we believe we should perform emotions, and bring into focus different aspects of emotion for consideration. In this way the different discourses we use create different possibilities for the ways we talk about emotion.

An autonomous discourse enabled Rita to use an elaborate language to describe her feelings, to locate them and to consider their personal effects. However, an autonomous discourse constrained our exploration of the relational and cultural contexts of Rita's feelings since she perceived emotions

Table 1.1 Comparing relational and autonomous emotion discourses

Relational	Autonomous
Inter-subjective Emotions are created between people: a social form of action to invite others to respond	**Subjective** Emotions are internal: an expression of something inside
Communal Emotions are shared and not bounded	**Personal** Emotions are an individual experience
Contextual We learn to do emotions and the appropriate situations to do them No separation of mind and body	**Bodily** Our emotions are the feelings inside our bodies Emotion is contrasted with reason
Focus on interpersonal relationships There is no direct correspondence between sensation and meaning. Emotions are distinguished according to relationships and meanings	**Focus on sensation** We think about our feelings (bodily sensation) with our minds. Emotions are classified according to body and facial expressions
Relate a narrative (process) Our emotion stories reflect an interweaving of the judgements we make about our sensations and actions in the contexts of our relationships	**Name a sensation (state)** The feelings are inside the body
Cultural We learn to do emotions as we live in cultures. Cultures have their local emotion grammars Therefore there is a wide range and number of emotions	**Innate and universal** We are born with emotions Emotions are universal There is a set number of core emotions

as internal to the individual and universal, 'I simply know ... everyone knows when they are bored'. The values and rules Desmond was using, on the other hand, limited his ability to distinguish or name his feeling in the workshop at all but did enable us to go on to explore the contexts of his emotion including his relationships with friends, family and work. His account of the ways in which his nursing culture informed his views that 'feelings from home' should be kept outside of the work place, reflects how our emotions are connected closely with culture and is coherent with a relational discourse that emotions need specific contexts for expression.

You may want to consider what aspects of autonomous and relational discourses of emotion you were using to reflect on your feeling at the start of this chapter. For example, did you view your feeling as a personal and subjective experience and something inside you which could or should be ventilated or expressed (autonomous discourse)? Or did you take a more communal view of the emotion as shared and created between people (relational discourse) and therefore not a specific attribute of only you? Were you focusing on the sensation of the emotion and making a clear distinction between mind and body (autonomous discourse)? Or were you focusing on interpersonal relationships in your emotion talk and reflecting on the emotion as a social form of action which invites others to respond (relational discourse)? Did you assume that emotions are innate, universal, easy to recognize and uncontrollable (autonomous discourse)? Or were you addressing the contexts of your emotion and perhaps relating cultural stories or rules reflecting your experience that emotions are closely connected with culture, gender, ethnicity, sexuality and class and that we learn to do them in our cultures (relational discourse)? Did your emotion talk tell a story about the sensations, actions, relationships and meanings of the emotion (relational discourse)? Or did you focus specifically on the sensation (autonomous discourse)?

In this book I adopt a relational approach to emotions informed by the relational discourses outlined above. In Chapter 7, I draw specific links between the relational practices described throughout the book and the language, values and rules that inform them.

Co-ordinating emotion talk

When we engage with each other in 'emotion talk' we are involved in a process of co-ordinating our actions and meanings so we can go on together. Our actions include the words we speak and the facial expressions, gestures, postures and voice tones we express through our bodies. In well co-ordinated emotion talk, our actions and meanings fit together well enough that all parties can create possibilities to go on in ways which they evaluate as satisfactory (Pearce, 1989). Sometimes we might refer to this satisfactory co-ordination as understanding each other or being understood. Poor co-ordination of emotion talk, on the other hand, creates experiences of confusion, frustration, blame, criticism or coercion.

Inviting Rita to name, describe and locate her feeling was sufficiently coherent with her autonomous discourse to enable us to co-ordinate well when we first engaged in emotion talk about her 'boredom'. Our conversation seemed to flow and we both experienced a satisfactory degree of mutual understanding. My questions addressing 'who else would have the same view on her emotions', or 'which relationship or circumstances might change the meaning or perspective of the emotion', however, did not make sense to Rita. These questions addressed relational aspects of her boredom and were incoherent with the personal, internal and universal views more consistent with the autonomous discourse she was using. We might call the latter part of our conversation an example of poor co-ordination that in other circumstances could have ended in experiences of confusion, frustration, blame or criticism.

Initially, Desmond could not answer any of my questions about his feelings since talking about his feelings was not coherent with the discourse of his nursing culture which prohibited talk about personal feelings in the work context. Although Desmond was keen to explore his 'interest', my connotation of his 'interest' as a 'feeling', at one point, created a degree of confusion and frustration between us and I was concerned about continuing lest Desmond experience my questions as coercion. However, Desmond and I were able to co-ordinate our emotion talk through co-creating a shared language, whereby our connotation of his 'interest' as an 'experience' rather than an 'emotion' or 'feeling' made it possible for us to go on in our conversation without challenging the emotion rules of his nursing culture.

Below, Grace, a clinical psychologist, shares with me in supervision an episode of interaction between herself, her manager and her colleague, Anne, in which she reported feeling frustrated and misunderstood in their emotion talk.

Whose feeling is it?

'Anne stopped me in the corridor in a state of urgency. She had to collect her son from school since he was not well. She had been planning to speak to our manager about a letter needing urgent attention and feared that if he did not deal with it she would have problems with an important aspect of her work. She was worried about her son and in a hurry and she urged me to get the severity of the matter concerning the letter across to our manager. Shortly afterwards I saw our manager in the same corridor. He was in a hurry and on his way to a meeting. I spoke to him quickly, emphatically and with a kind of pressure of speech hoping to get across the urgency of Anne's request. At our management meeting that afternoon, which Anne also attended, our manager asked me, "Grace, do you want to talk about your anxiety this morning?" I said, "Sorry – what?" because I genuinely did not know what he was talking about. So then he told me I had been very anxious that morning. I insisted I hadn't been but he just repeated again, "You were anxious, Grace". At this point I actually did begin to feel my body temperature rise and my heart race and I carried on, saying, "I was fine – I was only telling you what Anne asked me to. I was trying to make it clear she needed you to get that letter off before the deadline." He then said, "Crikey, what's going on here?" I was thinking, "You're the one who's anxious not me" when Anne piped up, "Well I was anxious actually".'

The emotion discourses we use help us to make sense of each other's communication. They also enable, allow, demand, prohibit or obligate us to respond in certain ways and offer a rationale for our actions. Therefore the extent and quality of how we co-ordinate our emotion talk is influenced by how our emotion 'world views' fit. Our emotion talk can become muddled or problematic when we are trying to co-ordinate with others informed by emotion rules and values incompatible with our own. In the conversation above we might assume that Grace and her manager were informed by different discourses in their emotion talk. Perhaps the manager was acting out of an autonomous discourse since he attributed the anxiety to a characteristic or property within Grace or to an expression of something inside of her ('your anxiety', 'you were anxious'). He also seemed to attribute himself certain rights and perhaps even responsibility or obligation to name and explain Grace's feeling and possibly even to teach her about her feeling. Grace's talk, on the other hand, reflects a relational discourse of emotion. Intending to move her manager by talking with feeling, she tried to use her body posture and voice to display the affect which would convey her colleague's urgency, 'I spoke … with a kind of pressure of speech hoping to get across the urgency of Anne's request', 'I was trying to make it clear…'.

The co-ordination of our emotion talk is not dependent on the quality of the discourse used by one participant alone. Rather it relates to how the fit between the language, values, rules and beliefs we are using helps or hinders our ability to enter into conversations about emotion with each other, co-ordinate our feelings and be together in emotion. For Rita, using an autonomous discourse did not enable her to make sense of my relational questions and we were not able to create enough of a fit in the latter part of our conversation to enable us to go on in our emotion talk. Desmond and I, on the other hand were able to create a suitable fit so that we could go on to discuss his 'interest'. Grace and her manager were informed by incommensurate emotion theories in their emotion talk so that both felt misunderstood and experienced their conversation as confusing, frustrating or coercive.

When the paediatric nurses asked me to see Junior A and his mother, below, to help them understand what he was feeling, I was wondering what emotion discourses were informing their abilities to talk and co-ordinate feelings with Junior and his mother.

An invitation to a different discourse

Nine-year-old Junior A was a patient on the paediatric ward. He had not spoken for three days and was refusing to eat. He had had his left leg amputated below the knee following a road traffic accident in which he had been knocked off his bicycle and run over on a pedestrian crossing. I learnt that the nursing team had accounted for Junior's withdrawal in terms of 'his anger' and that they had shared this explanation with Junior and his mother. Junior, however, remained silent. His mother continued to try and coax him to eat and speak and the nurses continued to feel frustrated and helpless. The nurses asked me to help Junior express his anger.

The nurses had tried to work with Junior and his mother using a number of practices informed by an autonomous discourse of emotion. They began by naming and explaining Junior's feeling, for example 'Maybe you're feeling a bit angry today', 'Junior is grieving since he misses his leg' or 'Maybe he is angry because he knows it is not fair that this has happened to him'. However, asking Junior what he felt and guessing or interpreting his feeling had resulted in Junior's continued silence. The nurses had also tried facilitating expression of Junior's feeling by suggesting, 'It's fine for both of you to have a good cry or even to get cross with us' or 'If you let it out of your system you'll feel a lot better'. They had also attempted educating or teaching the child and his mother about the right or wrong way to feel, for example, 'It's quite natural to feel angry when you have lost something important to you'. However, none of these autonomous practices helped Junior or his mother and seemed to be interfering with the nurses' relationship with Junior who pointedly ignored them and remained silent.

Hence considering an alternative to the autonomous and internalizing discourse of 'Junior's anger', whereby the feeling was identified as internal to the child ('Junior is angry', 'his anger'), I decided to adopt practices consistent with a relational discourse. In Chapter 2, I describe how I approach co-creating a name or meaning of the feeling with Junior, his mother and his carers instead of trying to provide a definitive description of the feeling from an expert position. Here I will describe another relational practice whereby I invited Mrs A and the nurses to approach what Junior was doing as a communication and hence an invitation. With Junior present I therefore asked them, 'If we look at what Junior is doing at the moment as an invitation from him to us to do something different, what might he be inviting us to do or say?' This question opened space for a very different sort of conversation between the ward team and Mrs A.

The nurse in charge thought Junior was 'calling for attention' and other nurses said the problem was that we had not worked out the sort of attention he wanted. The play specialist suggested Junior might want some explanations about what had happened to his leg and some understanding of what was going to happen, like when he would start walking again. Mrs A thought Junior might like some of his computer games from home and agreed with the play specialist's idea that he would want to know what was going to happen.

During this conversation, I noted that Junior's posture was markedly different. He appeared to be following the conversation carefully, focusing intently on each speaker as if with interest. At the end of the discussion, I therefore suggested we try responding to some of the ideas put forward, as an experiment, and that we monitor whether any of our responses made a difference to Junior.

The next time I met with Junior and his mother he was busily engaged in a complicated computer game. His mother said he had started eating again and that the physiotherapist had just told her 'he was the best in the class'. Junior beamed, although he did not lift his head from the game. The nurses said Junior 'was still not the most communicative child on the ward' and the play specialist said he had 'made a friend in the school room'.

Different discourses inform how we act and interact with others in emotion. Consistent with an autonomous discourse of emotion, the nurses were conceiving of Junior's feeling as internal and an expression of something inside of him. Hence they asked me to help him express or ventilate the feeling so that he could get rid of it, deal with it or perhaps get in touch with it. Since adopting autonomous practices of naming the feeling, ascribing it personally to Junior and attempting to teach him and his carers how best to deal with it, had not been successful, I moved towards relational practices with Junior and his carers. Attending to the relationship context of Junior's emotion, I therefore asked questions about the intended communication of his behaviour and expressions.

From colonization to co-creation

By distinguishing autonomous and relational practices, I recognize that I risk coercing you, the reader, to create an either/or dichotomy and perhaps even to feel the need to affiliate yourself with one or other 'side'. This is not my intention. First, I have learnt that people do not necessarily use only one discourse exclusively in their emotion talk. They may have access to a number of discourses and privilege different discourses in certain situations. You may already have noted, for example, that Desmond was probably using aspects of autonomous and relational discourses informed by his culture, training and gender in his emotion talk in the context of our workshop. His focus on the contexts of his relationships with his family and nursing culture, and his lack of attention to the sensation of his feeling, are consistent with a relational discourse. His unwillingness to attribute 'interest' as a feeling, on the other hand, might reflect his view that there is a core set of feelings that do not include 'interest' or that feelings are personal and individual. Second, I am not proposing that one discourse is superior to another. At the time I was working with Junior A and his carers, I had begun to privilege a relational discourse and relational practices in my work with people and feelings and you may therefore detect something of my 'promoting' relational practices in this account of my work. One might say I was becoming passionately attached to a relational discourse with the risk of dismissing the autonomous practices favoured by many staff and parents with whom I met until I was challenged in conversations with Denise and her daughter Anya below.

Respecting fear

Denise brought her six-year-old daughter, Anya, for help because Anya was afraid of going upstairs on her own. For example, she would cry and cling to her mother at the mere suggestion that she venture upstairs alone to fetch a jumper. This made bedtimes a particularly difficult time for all members of the family since it meant Anya's older sister, nine-year-old Kelly, had to go up to bed at the same time as her younger sister, which all members of the family, including Anya, considered was 'not fair'.

When I asked what people were doing to help the situation, Denise explained she had been encouraging Anya to 'talk about her fears' since she did not want her to 'hold on to anything that would upset her later on in life'. I asked Denise to help me understand her theory about fears. I explained that there are many theories about how to manage fears and that I wanted to learn how her 'talking theory' worked. Denise told me it was 'bad to keep feelings in'. When she was a child, herself, no one had ever been interested in her feelings. Her father was 'too busy working or out with his friends' and her mother was 'sweet but didn't have a clue'. Denise was committed to always being available for her children who knew they could tell her about their feelings any time.

From Denise's explanation I assumed that an autonomous discourse of emotion was informing her approach to feelings with her children and thereby shaping her attempts to sort out the current problems the family was having with fear. Denise had identified the fear as Anya's personal feeling, 'her fear'; as an expression of something internal, 'keep feelings in', and hence considered talking about the fear with Anya as a means of ventilating or getting it out. I also assumed that the autonomous discourse informing Denise's relationship with the fear was not useful to Denise and her family since she reported that talking about the fear had not yet helped Anya to manage her fear and thereby to go upstairs alone. Drawing from a relational discourse of emotion that construes emotions as created between people and therefore shared and not bounded, I hence invited all family members to come to a next meeting to help us think about ways of 'tackling this fear together'. I also suggested Anya involve her sister Kelly in some joint research to find out how other people they knew dealt with fear. Thus I was moving away from an internal ascription of the fear as inside and personal to Anya towards an externalization of the fear as something 'outside' of her so that she and her family might develop different sorts of relationship with this fear (White, 1989a,b). I describe the process of externalization in more detail in Chapter 7.

At our next meeting each family member presented with a number of good ideas to tackle fears. Anya's father, Mike, said he would avoid frightening situations. For example, he had not gone to a football match since the Hillsborough disaster. When I asked what he did if he had to face scary situations he could not avoid, he said he would sit down and think about it, try to understand why he was frightened and talk to himself about a reasonable way to counteract the fear. Denise said she always liked to talk to someone and to share her fear. Kelly told us that her friend had shown her that 'scary dogs leave you alone if you laugh when you walk past them'; she had tried it and it worked. Anya said her baby brother, Michael, could not tell her how to fight fear because he could not speak but she saw him 'run to cuddle mummy' if he was frightened. Kelly said their hamsters, Binkle and Flip, 'froze dead still' when they were really scared.

Anya and Kelly keenly agreed to write all these ideas down in a book (Durrant, 1990) that we later entitled *How to Shrink Fears by Anya and Kelly*, and they illustrated it beautifully in colour. At our next meeting we drew a 'staircase to fighting fear'. With Anya in charge, we worked out what she could be doing on the lower (least frightening) stairs to prepare herself, and then what facing fear on the top stairs would involve. Anya chose to put 'listening to story tapes upstairs in bed by myself' at the topmost step.

We all went on to discuss the pros and cons of the different methods of fighting fear the girls had documented in their book. Anya was very enthusiastic to participate in this conversation as if pleased to be forearmed with a set of possible manoeuvres to tackle fears. I responded rather enthusiastically to Kelly's laughing method, sharing that I had learnt from other children that fears shrink and look very silly when laughed at.

When Denise and Anya returned three weeks later, Anya was pleased to report that she was going upstairs on her own quite easily and was already listening to story tapes on her own in her room in the daytime. Denise said that she had sometimes heard Anya saying 'ha ha ha' while she was upstairs alone. Although Anya seemed very pleased with herself and quickly settled down to add artistic touches to the book on shrinking fear, I got the impression something was not quite right for Denise. When I asked her views on Anya's progress, Denise sighed and said she did 'not feel comfortable with it at all'. She was concerned we were 'teaching Anya to deny her feelings', in particular she worried that 'laughing off fear was encouraging her to be untrue to her real feelings'.

Denise's dissatisfaction highlighted how my enthusiasm for 'tackling fear' had engaged her husband and children but had inadvertently dismissed her strongly held view that 'fear is telling us something is wrong inside ... we need to pay it attention not laugh it off'. To avoid further coercion or colonization of Denise's emotion talk, therefore, I asked if she would help me learn more about her preferred theory of fear, in particular her view that a child should not be encouraged to 'laugh off fear'. Denise visibly relaxed when I asked, with curiosity, for examples of situations where it would be in Anya's interest to focus on the fear, pay it attention and listen to it. From her explanations, I tentatively summarized that 'the fear was telling us to pay attention to something ... like a sort of warning ... so there are times when it is important that we respect fear?'. Since Denise was pleased with my understanding, I went on to ask Anya when fear had warned her in a way that was good or helpful.

> *Glenda:* So when has it been good to listen to fear Anya? When has it helped you to take it seriously and listen to it?
>
> *Anya:* When I was at recorder class.
>
> *Glenda:* Oh? What happened?
>
> *Anya:* All the lights went out. It was dark and we couldn't see. It was scary. I didn't like it.
>
> *Glenda:* No? So what happened? What did fear do?
>
> *Anya:* I couldn't move in my chair. I was stuck in my chair.
>
> *Glenda:* Fear held you there? Were you [turning to her drawings in her book and pointing] freezing like Binkle and Flip here? Or [turning the pages and pointing] were you more like sitting still and trying to think and understand like Dad, here?
>
> *Anya:* [pointing at her drawing of the hamster] Like Binkle ... yeah.
>
> *Glenda:* Oh, [referring to an earlier discussion about the hamsters] is that like uhm ... so scared you were frozen ... but uhm ... watching and waiting for when it's safe to move again?
>
> *Anya:* [nodding] Mrs Arthur [music teacher] said all the children must sit very still and not move so she can get us a light.
>
> *Glenda:* Oh. So fear helped you stay really still until Mrs Arthur came back with a light? I suppose she wanted you all to stay still so she could know you would all be safe?
>
> *Anya:* Mmm. Some of the girls giggled like mad.
>
> *Glenda:* Really?
>
> *Anya:* I think they were trying to laugh it away.

Denise, Anya and I continued to discuss how and when we might decide to pay attention to fear, talk about it, and listen to its warnings and when we might decide that 'enough was enough', 'laugh it away' or use other means to shrink it or sort it. Denise seemed pleased with this conversation. At a final session without Anya, she told me she had realized she did not have many ways to deal with 'my own fears' and that she had learnt something for herself from our meetings.

Exploring discourses in emotion talk

A good enough fit between our emotion discourses is likely to enable a comfortable co-ordination and coherence in our emotion talk and feeling together. On the other hand, when our emotion discourses are incompatible, we are unlikely to understand each other's emotion language or create shared meanings with each other and more likely to experience each other's communications as an affront, oppressive or constraining. My work with Denise, Anya and family has taught me to pay careful attention to the emotion language, rules and theories of all the people in conversation with me so as to enable more co-ordinated rather than colonizing emotion talk. With this intention, I begin to explore Sheena's approach to feelings, below, paying attention to the language she is using and the theories and rules informing her emotion talk.

Feeling nothing

> Sheena came for help because she was worried she was 'not feeling anything' about her mother's recent deterioration with Parkinson's disease and consequent admission to a nursing home. When I asked how things would be for Sheena if 'not feeling anything' was not troubling her at that moment, she replied, 'I'm not unhappy ... otherwise I'm OK ... the problem is I'm not feeling anything ... I don't want to end up like my husband.' I learnt that Sheena's husband, Alan, had lost his father two years previously when he 'dropped dead suddenly' and that 'Alan carried on for six months as if nothing had happened and then fell apart'. According to Sheena, 'he bottled it all up – it all had to come out in the end.'

At the start of our talking together my intention was to understand and co-ordinate with Sheena's language, meanings, rules and theories of emotion. Therefore, in the following transcript I ask Sheena questions similar to those I asked you, the reader, at the start of this chapter with a view to exploring how she prefers to describe her experience with feeling and how she prefers to understand feeling and to engage in emotion talk. I ask Sheena to explain how she distinguishes the feeling (How would you know it was a feeling?); to name the feeling (If you were feeling something what would it be?) and whether and where she locates it (Where would the feeling be coming from?). I also invite her to consider the relational contexts of the feelings she describes (What would people notice of the feeling? How would you like people to respond to the feeling?). I anticipate that these sorts of questions will give me an idea of the discourses Sheena prefers to privilege in her emotion talk. For example, the questions could help me explore whether she perceives feelings as subjective or inter-subjective, innate and universal or cultural and whether she focuses on the sensation and/or the relational context of the feeling.

Glenda: Would it be OK, Sheena, if I ask you a few questions to help me understand a bit more about ... how it is for you ... not feeling anything at the moment? Is that OK?

Sheena: Yes, fine.

Glenda: So, can you help me understand – how do you make sense of your not feeling anything? What understanding do you have of this?

Sheena: Shock maybe ... shock ...

Glenda: If you were feeling something ... other than shock ... what would it be?

Sheena: Sadness ... maybe anger with my father.

Glenda: How would you know it was a feeling ... the anger or the sadness?

Sheena: I'd feel sick, tight ... not be able to sleep ... think about it all the time ... maybe unable to eat.

Glenda: Would you be experiencing these feelings anywhere in particular? Would there be a particular place, say, you'd be feeling them ... they'd be coming from ... Or not?

Sheena: My stomach. I'd feel it here. [Points to between her chest and her stomach]

Glenda: [Pointing to the place between my chest and stomach.] What is happening there at the moment? What does it feel like?

Sheena: [sighing] Numb ... nothing [looking deflated].

Glenda: So you're feeling numb?

Sheena: Yes.

Glenda: Does that feel like a good enough description, name for you – numb? Or do you prefer different words?

Sheena: Numb is fine.

Glenda: What sense are you making of the numb feeling?

Sheena: The shock? I don't know – maybe there's too much at the moment.

Glenda: Too much to feel?

Sheena: [nods]

Glenda: Is numb the only feeling you have these days – the main one?

Sheena: [nods]

Glenda: So what would I notice if you were feeling something like sadness or anger? Instead of ... say – numb?

Sheena: I'm not sure you would notice anything. I don't know, maybe I would look sad.

Glenda: Would I see it then … this feeling?

Sheena: Well I do show a lot through my body – I get very slouchy when I'm low.

Glenda: And others, your family? Who would be most likely to notice you feeling this way?

Sheena: I don't know. I suppose Alan would notice I was down. But it would be me feeling it not him, so he wouldn't know what I was feeling – not exactly.

Glenda: How would you like Alan to respond to these feelings – say sadness … or anger?

Sheena: I don't know. Hmmm … I must say I haven't thought about him or the children noticing what I feel – or them doing much about it. Hmmm … I wouldn't want them to have to take it all on board. It would be my sadness – you know – about my mum, not their responsibility.

Glenda: You would see it as your feelings and not their responsibility?

Sheena: [nods] I haven't thought about them noticing …

From our conversation above I notice Sheena is privileging certain language, rules and theories in her emotion talk. For example, it seems important for her to identify a bodily feeling and to name it, 'I'd feel sick, tight …' in the 'stomach'. She construes her feeling as an individual and personal sensation, 'it would be me feeling it', 'my sadness', and perhaps she assumes a core set of universal feelings which include 'sadness' and 'anger' but possibly not 'numb'. I also note Sheena finds my questions about the relational contexts of her feelings different, 'I haven't thought about him or the children noticing what I feel'. Sheena appears to be interested in thinking about the effect of her feelings and the meanings of her emotional expression for other people in her family. Therefore I contemplate that she might be curious to participate with me further in aspects of a relational discourse and describe this conversation further in Chapter 2.

In therapeutic conversations we might offer or introduce a different discourse or metaphors of emotion as I did with Junior A, his mother and ward staff and attempted with Denise and her family above. On the other hand we might 'join' the emotion language (see Chapter 2) and enter into the discourse of the people with whom we are talking, as I have tried to do with Sheena above. We might also work towards co-creating a new, shared discourse with a view towards transforming emotions through our emotion talk. In Chapter 2, I go on with curiosity and questioning to invite Sheena to extend the discourse we are using in our emotion talk so that we might elaborate or transform more enabling emotions without undermining or colonizing the discourses that inform her preferred sense of self, culture and community.

CHAPTER 2
Naming emotions

At the start of Chapter 1, I invited you, the reader, to name and describe the feeling you were having in the moment (What feeling do you have now as you are reading these words? Describe the feeling). I then went on to explore how you distinguished the feeling you had identified by asking how you knew whether this was a feeling or not (How do you know you are feeling what you describe? How would I know you are feeling this way?). Perhaps you would like to reflect on whether you were easily able to identify and name a feeling and what was informing your ability to do so. Were you readily able to identify and name a feeling like Rita who felt 'bored' at the start of the workshop? Were you reluctant to name an emotion, like Desmond who considered it inappropriate to 'discuss your feelings at work'? Were you unable to distinguish an emotion at all like Sheena who initially complained of 'feeling nothing' but 'numb' in a therapy consultation?

Different theories address whether it is possible or, indeed, useful to distinguish and name our own emotions or those of others. In 1872 Charles Darwin proposed that it was possible to identify a 'core set' of universally recognizable emotions, and many others since have assumed a common 'core set' of emotions, although the 'core' emotions identified have varied considerably. For example, Tomkins (1962) described nine 'innate affects': interest–excitement, enjoyment–joy, surprise–startle, fear–terror, distress–anguish, anger–rage, 'dismell', disgust and shame–humiliation. Ekman (1989) identified happiness, sadness, anger, surprise, disgust and fear, and Oatley and Johnson-Laird (1996) reported nine 'basic emotions', four which can be experienced without a cause: happiness, sadness, anger and fear, plus five which are object-related: attachment, parental love, sexual attraction, disgust and personal rejection. When Sheena came for help because she was feeling nothing (Chapter 1), it was as though she was saying she had no emotion. Perhaps she was assuming a 'core set' of emotions which did not include the 'numb' or 'shock' which reflected her experience at that time.

Giving words to emotions creates several opportunities. It can enable people to communicate and create understanding with each other. It can also make it easier to discuss what relationship a person wants to have with a feeling. For example, creating a name for Sheena's feeling opened space for Sheena and I to discuss what relationship she wanted to have with her feelings 'numb' and 'shock' and to explore the effects of her feelings on her relationships with her family.

However, we cannot assume that language can accurately represent our emotion experience. As William James (1890) was pointing out, while Darwin was making a case for a 'core set' of universal emotions, there is considerable variation in the ways people express similar named feelings so that some people might cry where others might laugh. Since James others have noted that it is not possible to accurately and directly correlate emotions with specific physiological conditions (Averill, 1996) and that we can experience mixtures of emotions for which we do not have well-developed language (Oatley and Johnson-Laird, 1996). Therefore even when we do have a word for an emotion, the same word may be used and understood in different ways by different people, for example Grace's manager gave the name 'anxiety' to what Grace may well have called 'urgency'.

Creating a shared language and joint understanding of emotion

Since we cannot start from the position that we all share a common language of emotion that accurately transfers meanings and experiences between people, we need to approach the meaning of emotion words as uniquely related to the people we are talking with. To communicate meaningfully about our feelings with each other, we need to pay careful attention to the language and meanings people are using in the moment towards creating a shared language and understanding of emotions. In this book, therefore, I describe an approach to talking with people about emotion that moves away from trying to fit people's experience to a 'core set' of emotion names preselected by experts in the emotion field. Instead I suggest relational practices intended to bring forth or create with people ways of talking about emotion that enable them to describe their experience in ways that resonate for *them*. To create a shared language of emotion, therefore, I propose joining the language of the other, adopting an attitude of curiosity and exploring emotion words through the multiple contexts of the lives of the people I am communicating with.

Joining the language of the other

To join the language of others, I pay careful attention to the language already in use by those involved. By language, I mean both speech and actions, verbal and non-verbal communication. When I notice that people's preferred medium of communication is non-verbal, I usually invite them to show me (rather than tell me) about their feeling, for example, by creating opportunities for drawing, making or performing the feeling through a medium they feel comfortable with. I try to respond to their showing with an action coherent with their preferred medium of expression. For example, when people have shown me the size of their feelings I have responded by measuring or weighing them (Fredman, 1997).

> Elsewhere (Fredman, 1997), I describe my work with a 10-year-old boy called Jamie M who had stopped talking after he was told of the recurrence of a leukaemia he had battled against, in the face of gruelling treatments since the age of six. The doctors and nurses were very worried about 'how Jamie was feeling' since, formerly a lively boy, he had withdrawn from them. Since I knew Jamie liked modelling with clay, I invited him to make a model of his feeling. Jamie and his father produced an ornate sculpture the following day. It resembled a solid rectangle with branches that were connected by a sort of web of strings.
>
> Thus I began by inviting Jamie to demonstrate his 'feeling' through his preferred medium of expression, modelling clay. I then offered him the opportunity to choose the name for his feeling. The following extract is reprinted with permission from Fredman (1997) Death Talk: Conversations with children and families, Karnac Books. London.

Glenda: Does this feeling have a name?

Jamie: [shakes his head]

Glenda: If it did have a name, what would you call it?

Jamie: [rolls his tongue against his top palate and lips making a sound something like balup-balup]

[Mr M laughed. Jamie grinned]

Glenda: Is balup-balup around you at the moment, Jamie?

Jamie: [nods]

Glenda: Do you like feeling balup-balup?

[Again Jamie shrugged]

Glenda: Do you want to keep balup-balup, get rid of it, shrink it, grow it or something else?

Jamie: Control it.

Glenda: Is balup-balup troubling you now or do you have it under control?

Jamie: [looking at his sculpture, then at his father] Today I'm the controller.

Glenda: I see ... so what helps you to control balup-balup?

Jamie: When Dad is here.

Glenda: Mr M how do you help Jamie control balup-balup?

Mr M: [smiling] I have no idea, no idea.

Jamie: Tells me I can do things.

If names are already being used to describe an emotion, I clarify whether the words in use are preferred and whether they provide a suitable description for the people involved. My intention is always to participate in the creation of words that describe people's experience in ways that resonate and fit best for them. For example, in the previous chapter, one could have explained to Sheena that she was denying her feelings and told her what she was feeling or would feel in the circumstance. Rather than preselecting from a limited range of assumed emotions informed by my preferred emotion theories however, I was curious about Sheena's unique ways of experiencing and describing emotions. Therefore I asked questions intending to open space for her to elaborate a vocabulary to describe her emotional experience which resonated for her. My intention was to join her in her choice of language. For example, asking Sheena what sense she made of 'not feeling anything', generated her response, 'shock'. Inviting her to identify and describe the sensation of the 'shock' and to locate it brought forth a further naming of 'numb'. Thus unconstrained by whether the words she used were conforming to a previously prescribed or recognized 'core set' of emotions, I tentatively invited Sheena to use her own words, 'shock' and 'numb', to identify her feeling, 'So you're feeling numb? ... Does that feel like a good enough description for you – feeling numb – or do you prefer different words?'

In a similar way, rather than ignore Jamie's word, 'balup-balup', treat it as nonsense or try to establish the underlying meaning of it, the nurses and I explored how Jamie preferred to use 'balup-balup' with us. We referred continually to Jamie's expertise on the word's uses and how best to respond to it with questions like 'What is 'balup-balup' up to today? What would you like to do for/with balup-balup now?'. Therefore instead of receiving Jamie's chosen word, 'balup-balup', as nonsense, we embraced it in pursuit of its meaning and uses.

An utterance is only nonsense when we do not know how to go on to use it in a sensible or coherent way. To know the meaning of a word, then, is to know how to use it and how to respond to it in a particular context (Wittgenstein, 1953). In this way the meaning of a feeling word emerges in its use and we need to attend constantly to the context of the person expressing this feeling without making assumptions. When language is approached as a form of action rather than a form of representation, in this way, meanings and understandings tend to emerge and change in the course of interactions. It is therefore not necessary to ensure that all persons have exactly the same understanding of the utterance or symbol. What is necessary is that we develop abilities to co-ordinate our language and actions with each other, thereby co-creating local meanings (Lyotard, 1984) of the expressions in ways that make sense and allow us to go on. In Chapter 6, I develop this approach to emotions as actions, addressing how we might join people in the performance of their feelings rather than interpret what they stand for or refer to.

Within our cultures and families we ascribe value and meaning to emotions, for example whether they are positive or negative, desirable or unwanted, suitable or unsuitable. To join with people's language of emotion and to share and extend our meanings, we might therefore explore the values they attribute to the emotion words we are using. For example, I could have asked Sheena, 'Could you help me understand a bit more about this numb? What kind of numb is it? Is it a good numb or not so good? Is the numb mixed with any other kind of feelings?' In this way we might look for what is 'inside the word' for the person who speaks. Tom Andersen (1995) explains that looking for what is 'inside the word' is not looking for what is 'behind' the word or 'under' the word. To look behind or under the word involves taking an interpretative and possibly expert position on the words of the other – seeing what we see and not what they say or experience. Tom Andersen gives further examples of the sorts of questions I could have asked to look 'inside' Sheena's emotion words like: 'If you were to look for something else in this word "shock", what would you find?'; 'If "numb" could speak what would the words be?'; 'What would we see if we walked inside that word?'

Below I learn the meaning of the word 'anger' for Lorna. She also tells me what it is like to have her feelings named and identified unilaterally by someone else.

> Lorna had been diagnosed with multiple sclerosis six years ago. She was permanently confined to a wheelchair and had lost some fine motor use of her hands. Prior to this conversation, Lorna and I had been talking about the diet she was following in an attempt to control her symptoms. She had adhered rigorously to a macrobiotic diet for three years. She was still having relapses of the multiple sclerosis and had begun to doubt the efficacy of the diet. She had spoken of herself as 'cheating' on the diet and said she preferred my construction of her eating what she wanted as 'indulging' herself.

Lorna: People are always asking me if I am angry because I have MS.

Glenda: [Thinking Lorna had said 'hungry' which sounded like 'ungry' to my ear untuned to Lorna's accent which was quite different from my own] Why? Why should you be?

Lorna: Exactly – I don't know …

Glenda: Because of the diet you mean?

Lorna: Why – diet?

Glenda: I don't know, I was thinking maybe they think you're hungry because …

Lorna: [interrupting] I don't get hungry on the diet – why would that make me angry?

Glenda: Angry? I thought you said hungry …

Lorna: Not hungry – angry!

[Both laughing]

I have decided to include this part of our conversation here since it reflects something of the process we often go through when trying to find names that are acceptable and understandable for people involved in the process of co-creating emotions. In this example it was my mishearing Lorna's description of 'angry' as 'hungry' which nearly interrupted our ability to have a mutually coherent conversation about her emotion. It is not uncommon, however, even when we hear the words correctly, for us to create similar misunderstandings of each other's emotion language, and thereby undermine our ability to go on meaningfully in our emotion talk. My attempts to join Lorna's language, adopt a posture of curiosity about her feeling 'hungry' and share her meanings of 'hungry' helped us to clarify and negotiate a mutually meaningful language. Hence we could go on together to discuss the effect on her of being described as 'angry'.

Glenda: So what's that like for you – people asking you if you're angry?

Lorna: [laughing] It makes me furious … [laughing further, apparently at the irony]. They really think I am [angry]. Why should I be?

Glenda: [laughing with her] Does it help?

Lorna: What?

Glenda: Well there is the idea that giving a name to feelings can help to …

Lorna: [raising the pitch of her voice] No – it gives me a feeling – not a … name …

Glenda: How do you mean?

Lorna: It makes me angry.

Glenda: Oh – asking if you're angry – suggesting it – makes you angry?

Lorna: Yes [laughing]

Glenda: So the asking makes the feeling?

Lorna: Exactly – makes it – huh …

Lorna shows how language not only describes her reality but can create it when she recounts how other people's bringing forth 'anger' as a description of *her* self *makes* the feeling. Thus the words we use can shape our experience and our futures and in this way can become constitutive of life itself. In this situation Lorna does not like the attribution of 'anger' and goes on to give us some understanding of the effect of being attributed an emotion name that does not fit.

Glenda: And how does the suggestion that you might feel angry – how does that affect you – uh what …

Lorna: Not great.

Glenda: In what way … does it … how does it make … how does it affect what you do or …

Lorna: Well I end up feeling bad about feeling angry.

Glenda: Bad? Can you explain why bad with angry?

Lorna: Nobody likes to be seen as angry … would you?

When I am asked to name the emotion on behalf of a client, I rarely find that my autonomous naming of the person's feeling alone enables people to find a way to go on or positively enhances our communication. I now wonder how many times I have unwittingly created 'bad' feelings for people, akin to Lorna's experience of the unwanted 'angry' attribution, by naming a feeling without fully understanding the meanings and implications of that naming for the people involved. Lorna's account encourages me to start from the position that only clients themselves can access their immediate experience. I also assume I cannot know the meaning of the emotion word a client is using and a client cannot know the meaning of an emotion word I might use without talking about it. My intention therefore is to get as near to the client's experience of feeling through our talking together, to enter into the client's world of meaning and experience by asking questions.

Adopting an attitude of curiosity

To enter into the client's meaning and experience I adopt an attitude of 'curiosity' (Cecchin, 1987) rather than 'certainty' in our emotion talk. An attitude of certainty would involve my providing a definitive description of the client's feeling from an expert position, assuming a 'true' definition of the feeling to which I, as expert, had primary access. Adopting an attitude of curiosity, on the other hand, involves putting aside my assumptions about what clients are feeling or what word most fits their experience in that moment and concentrating on listening to what they are saying and showing. Rather than expecting to discover information or facts about their emotions, I anticipate that understanding will evolve in the course of our conversation. Therefore I ask questions to invite people's descriptions of their experience and meanings and then allow their talk to guide my listening and talking. In this way I am trying to 'talk-in-order-to-listen' rather than to 'listen-in-order-to-talk' (Lyotard, 1979; Shawver, 2001). I encourage people to develop their responses to my questions fully, taking the position that they are the 'primary interpreters of their own experience' (Freedman and Combs, 1996). I take the position that I always need to be informed by the other for understanding to develop. Thus I am working at asking questions that open rather than close conversation, not understanding too quickly, being open to the unexpected and avoiding valuing my own knowing over that of the client (Anderson and Goolishian, 1992).

To avoid dominating Junior A, his mother and the nursing team (Chapter 1) with one of my preferred emotion discourses, therefore, I began by trying to join with their language. Since the nurses were using the term 'anger' liberally in communication with Junior and his mother, I began with the same word they were using. However, I did not assume that 'anger' was the preferred description for all of them or that the meanings and experiences I associated with 'anger' were the same as the meanings and experiences they might associate with it. Therefore I set out, from a position of curiosity to explore what 'anger' meant for each of them.

I asked questions about the effects of naming Junior's feeling as 'anger' on people and on relationships with a view to helping me get a closer understanding of their meanings and experience. For example, I asked:

How does seeing Junior as angry help you/him/the ward?

If Junior is helped to think of himself as angry what opportunities does it provide?

Are there ways that this description [angry] can get in the way of things or create difficulties for you/Junior?

If you choose to see Junior's silence and his not looking at the nurses as anger, how does it affect things between you/what you might do next/how you are with him?

Junior's mother Mrs A, said it would not help her or Junior if 'he was angry'. She felt she would be unable to help him and she could 'see no good come of it'. The nurses were divided about the opportunities a description of anger might provide. Whereas some of them believed helping Junior know he was angry would 'free him to express what he is feeling', others thought referring to anger had distanced them from both Junior and his mother.

Allowing their talk to guide my listening, gave us all the opportunity to learn that Mrs A wanted to help Junior in a way that 'good could come of it' and that the nurses recognized and were concerned about the distance developing between them and the family. These were unexpected understandings that emerged in the course of our conversation and that opened up opportunities for further understanding and helped communication to develop between the ward team and the family.

Taking care not to be guided by pre-selected emotion words or meanings, in this case 'anger' as selected by the nurses, I could have explored what alternative emotions they might create for Junior, and the associated consequences for meaning, relationships, and action of different emotion constructions by asking, for example:

– If you chose another feeling for Junior instead of anger, what might you choose?
– What feeling do you think Junior would like to choose for himself?

There are times when I do offer my own emotion descriptions when engaged in emotion talk with people, especially when people specifically ask me for my 'professional' opinion on 'what do I feel?'. In the course of our exploratory conversation I might offer emotion names, always tentatively, in the form of a question, for example, below I ask Jane, 'I was thinking like maybe – is there also a bit of admiration in this jealousy with Linda?' In an attempt to avoid imposing my emotion descriptions as correct or definitive, however, I also explore how this description fits for the people involved by asking what effect this description would have on relationships, actions, and views of self and others.

Exploring emotion words through the contexts of people's lives

We learn the meaning of emotion words by attending to the sum of the contexts in which the words are used (Lutz, 1985). Thus our different contexts inform the meanings we give to feelings. These contexts include the cultures of our ethnicity, gender, age, religion, sexuality and the cultures of our families and professional training. Therefore our emotions are shaped by our cultures and we learn to 'do' emotions as we live in our cultures.

Our vocabularies of emotion are created in and handed down through our cultures. The more an emotion is valued, whether it be positively or negatively, the more likely it is to be recognized and named so we might expect each culture to have its own different 'core emotions' which are attributed specific values and meaning within that culture. The naming and classification of emotions does differ considerably between different cultures, for example, even the numbers of words used to describe emotions varies – in Chinese (Taiwanese) there are about 750 words whereas in English more than 400 terms have been identified as labels of emotional states (Heelas, 1996; Baron-Cohen, 2003). Also, emotions can vary within a culture over time, with new emotions emerging while others disappear (Stearns and Knapp, 1996). Hence our abilities to describe and experience an emotion can be enabled or constrained by our cultural vocabularies (Gergen, 1999). In this way our cultures inform the ways in which we distinguish and name our own emotions and those of others and can influence our actual experience of emotion as well as our emotion talk.

I learnt much of my early 'emotioning' at the interface of two cultures. I grew up in a white Jewish family in Africa and was cared for during the day by Emmah Gumede, an Ndebele woman. Emmah came from a royal family and embraced her cultural values with pride. Therefore I was privileged to have the opportunity for Emmah's culture to play a significant part in the early shaping of my emotions.

Just 'jeh'

When I was about three or four Emmah was supervising my little friend Tessa and me as we played on the garden swing. Having had my turn, I had to stand and watch as Emmah pushed Tessa high in the air. What stands out in my memory is my hysterical crying and squealing as I wanted my turn and my mother calling out, in concern, 'What is happening to the little one?' I vividly remember the quality of Emmah's soothing, singsong voice and her words, 'Nothing – don't worry – she's just jeh'. I heard those same words used many times in different contexts to describe my experience or the behaviour of others, for example, when I complained tearfully of my sister's teasing, always with the same reassuring tone and cadence of voice, Emmah explained her behaviour, 'Don't worry she's just jeh'. In the course of my early years the message I took was something like 'this is tolerable', 'don't pay this too much attention' and 'this will pass'. 'Just jeh' became a concept we incorporated into our family emotion talk that over time was renamed 'just jealous'. It kept its reassuring 'this will pass' connotation.

I have continued to develop my relationship with jealousy through the different contexts of my life beyond my relationship with Emmah and my childhood family relationships. My professional context is one that has shaped what jealousy has come to mean for me.

I had not been living long in Britain when I exclaimed, 'I am so jealous!' out of admiration and with intended congratulations to a colleague who announced that she had received a research travel award. I was met with a look of concerned surprise from my colleague.

It appeared that for this colleague I was not 'just jeh' and that she might have been anticipating something of an 'envious attack' like Jane describes below.

> I had met with Jane, a university teacher, on two occasions. She had sought my help for what she described as her 'difficulty making friends'. At our third meeting Jane complained she could not work with her colleague, Linda, since 'Linda is jealous of me'. I asked Jane, 'How do you know she is jealous?' and learnt, 'She is always watching me, she competes with me – always doing exactly what I'm doing. And she compliments me all the time – I don't believe her.'

My question, 'What's wrong with that – if Linda is jealous of you?' created an opening for Jane and me to explore some of the contexts informing her relationship with jealousy.

Jane: I don't know, I don't like it.

Glenda: Jealousy? Or – uh compliments?

Jane: [smiling] No – but I see what you are getting at – no jealousy.

Glenda: Jealousy – why not? How come you don't like it? What's wrong with it? What effect does it have on you?

Jane: It frightens me. Um yeah – frightens me.

Glenda: Frightens you? I see. Do you have a sense of what you are frightened of – like what would happen or something like that?

Jane: I don't know. I feel like I've been protecting myself from people's jealousy all my life. [Laughing] I've made a bit of a career of it.

Glenda: As well as your academic career? Have you been as successful?

Jane: [laughs] I wouldn't say it's got me anywhere.

Glenda: No? So where does this idea come from – that jealousy is frightening? Who told you this?

Jane: No one told me in that way. I picked it up along the way.

Glenda: How? Where from?

Jane: In my family mainly. My mother was envious of me. She was always telling me how lucky I was to have everything she didn't get as child. That she could have done better than me if she had got what I had. And my older sister was always taking my clothes and insisting they were hers. My mother always let her. They would gang up on me – tell me I was spoilt. It was hideous.

Glenda: Can you help me understand. Where does the jealousy fit in here?

Jane: They were jealous of me – that I achieved more than my mother – and that I was prettier than my sister I suppose.

Glenda: So is it that sort of jealousy that frightens you?

Jane: [nods]

Glenda: What sort of jealousy would you call it?

Jane: [Taking time to find the word] Undermining ... mmm ... undermining ...

Glenda: Undermining? And the kind Linda is showing – is it also undermining? Or are there other – um sort of bits like ... other ingredients in there? Or is it all undermining?

Jane: I don't think I get you.

Glenda: I don't know – I was thinking – maybe is there also a bit of admiration in this jealousy with Linda?

Exploring the meaning of emotion words through the different contexts of people's lives creates opportunities for sharing and extending meanings together. Having explored 'jealousy' in the context of her family relationships, Jane and I go on, below, to explore the meaning of 'jealousy' and 'admiration' in the context of her relationship with her colleague Linda. When I had wondered whether there was a 'bit of admiration' in the jealousy Jane attributed to Linda, Jane had seemed surprised, 'Admiration? What makes you think that?' I therefore invited Jane to consider what opportunities a description of 'admiration' might offer and what constraints it might pose to her in the context of her relationship with Linda.

Glenda: If you choose to describe Linda's behaviour as jealousy ...

Jane: Jealousy?

Glenda: If we stay with jealousy for a moment ... so choosing to describe Linda as jealous ... how does that affect what you do – or how you are with Linda?

Jane: Like I said, I withdraw, keep my distance.

Glenda: And how is that for you? Do you prefer to withdraw? Is that OK for you?

Jane: Mmm ... it doesn't help much .... uh ...

Glenda: Not help you – or what? Could you explain a bit more to help me understand?

Jane: Well that's what I meant when I said I've been doing this all my life.

Glenda: Making a career of withdrawing?

Jane: [nods]

Glenda: So are you saying that describing Linda as jealous is not helping you much – you withdraw and you don't like doing this ... being like this?

Jane: [nods] No ... I don't.

Glenda: What if you saw Linda as admiring – what would you be likely to do?

Jane: Admiring … I'd be … I'd …. I'd be a bit … wary.

Glenda: Wary? Is that the same as withdrawing?

Jane: No – no – it's different because I'd hang in there – you know what I mean? I wouldn't quite believe it.

Glenda: But you'd stay around to find out more?

Jane: Yes – I would …

Glenda: So how would that make things between you and Linda?

Jane: Better – wouldn't it? At least there'd be a chance of getting on – finding out at the very least. Well … the bottom line is we … I could work with her.

Exploring the story of a person's experience with feelings through the different contexts of that person's life helps us create richer understandings of his or her emotions. Asking Jane, 'So where does this idea come from – that jealousy is frightening? Who told you this?' opened space for her to recount how she acquired her abilities to approach jealousy within the context of her family. Thus learning something of the events that triggered jealousy in Jane's experience and how jealousy was approached in her family offered a multi-layered picture of Jane's experience and relationship to jealousy. Questions like, 'How do you know you/they are feeling what you describe?'; 'Who else would give it this name?'; 'Where do you get your ideas about this emotion from?'; 'Who else shares your views on this emotion?' can invite people to reflect on the contexts that inform their emotion and can bring forth conversations from their relationship, family and cultural contexts.

By joining me in an exploration of the contexts that shaped her relationship with jealousy, Jane began to transform her relationship with it. At first she was dominated by the fear engendered by this emotion and her associated connotation of jealousy as always 'undermining'. In the course of our conversation she moved towards a curiosity about other possible meanings of the emotion including 'admiration'. Like Jane, my relationship with jealousy has also elaborated over time. Extending beyond 'just jeh' it now includes connotations of the 'envious attack', 'admiration' and 'celebration', among others.

Above, I asked Jane questions intended to invite her to introduce the contexts informing her emotions, for example, 'So where does that idea come from – that jealousy is frightening? Who told you this?' In response Jane herself identified the context of her 'family'. She then went on to tell her story of jealousy which involved her mother and her sister, later adding that her father used to 'make excuses' for her mother and sister's treatment of her with the explanation that they were jealous of her.

At other times I may initiate the introduction of a context into our emotion talk with a client. For example, I introduced the contexts of Sheena's relationships with her children and her husband into our emotion talk, thereby opening space for Sheena to further explore the 'numb' she had been feeling in response to her mother's admission to a nursing home (Chapter 1). In the course of our conversation, Sheena then went on to notice feelings like 'irritable', 'pain' and later 'anger' as well as other 'unexpected' feelings.

Glenda: So have you been doing anything? Uh – with that numb – uh – how have you been ... say ... with Alan and the children?

Sheena: I have been really irritable – with the children – I shouted at Vicky.

Glenda: Irritable – is that a feeling – or ...?

Sheena: Uh – yes – and it was so painful leaving my mum behind – she looked so lost.

Glenda: Was that a feeling – or ...?

Sheena: [nods]

Glenda: So – um – pain?

Sheena: Mmm ...

Glenda: What about feeling irritable? Is it a feeling you prefer to numb?

Sheena: That's a strange question.

Glenda: It is rather – do you want to try and answer it or is it too strange – I have been told that some of my questions are not worth answering.

Sheena: No I didn't mean that – I'd like to try. What was it again?

Glenda: I was wondering whether you prefer the feeling irritable or numb?

Sheena: It's hard to say. I hate feeling numb – I don't feel alive and I know it's not good for me. But I feel lousy being irritable – it's not Vicky's fault, I shouldn't be taking it out on her.

Glenda: Are you saying you feel more alive though – when you're irritable and you think that's better for you?

Sheena: I'm not sure.

Glenda: You were saying you feel lousy when you see yourself as irritable?

Sheena: Mmm

Glenda: You mentioned Vicky – how does seeing yourself as irritable affect things between you and the children?

Sheena: I'm ratty with them – all the time – and then I feel mean, I can see it's not their fault.

Glenda: And numb – how does focusing on numb make things for you and the children?

Sheena: I can get on with things much easier – but – oh I don't know ...

Glenda: If you chose – if things were as you wanted them – how would you like things to be with you and the children and Alan?

Sheena: Like before.

Glenda: Before? How was that? You mentioned feeling alive and also getting on with things?

Sheena: We … I don't know … we were like a real family. We laughed and had fun …

Glenda: Did you also get irritable sometimes?

Sheena: Yes – and that – but it didn't get on top of me.

Glenda: So now I'm wondering about pain. Are there times when you prefer pain to numb? You mentioned feeling pain when you left your mum at the nursing home.

Sheena: It was so awful – that feeling – I couldn't bear … I couldn't survive if I felt like that all the time.

Glenda: The pain?

Sheena: Mmm

Glenda: So how are numb and pain and uh – irritable – how are they connected? What's the connection between them? I mean … how do they sort of … uh – can you feel them all at once for example …?

Sheena: Not sure

Glenda: Is numb the feeling that looks after pain – like a protection sort of feeling?

Sheena: Yes – but I shouldn't be protecting – it'll all catch up with me later – like with Alan …

Glenda: How is your situation different from Alan's?

Sheena and I continued to talk about the possibility that her mother might live with progressive disability for years. She began to ask herself how long any person could grieve and feel pain and to give herself permission to enjoy her relationships with her children. She also spoke of her 'anger' with her father for 'dumping' her mother in a nursing home and for the way he had treated her mother throughout Sheena's life. The following session she said she was having all sorts of feelings including ones she 'never expected'.

Sheena's evaluation of her feelings varied across the contexts of her relationships with her mother, her father, her children, her husband and herself. Initially she said she should be feeling 'sadness' or perhaps 'anger' but not 'numb' since it was 'not good for me'. However she did not like the effect of 'irritable' on her family relationships, especially her relationship with her daughter Vicky. When we brought in the context of time, in particular the future and the consideration that her mother may live for many years with the debilitating effects of a severe form of Parkinson's disease, her evaluation of her emotions changed yet again as she gave herself permission to enjoy her children.

Naming emotions is a powerful act

In this chapter we see how emotion words are able to make things happen. That is they do more than simply describe or refer to experiences, they can also create different sorts of relationships and realities. Thus naming a feeling can move people towards new positions, different roles and alternative ways of experiencing (Riikonen and Smith, 1997). For example, above, Jane shows how attributing the different names, 'jealousy' or 'admiration', to her colleague's emotion, creates different opportunities and constraints for their relationship. She explains how she withdraws from her colleague, Linda, when she attributes 'jealousy' to her behaviour whereas naming Linda's response as 'admiring' creates possibilities for a different sort of relationship in which she 'could work with her'. Lorna shows how naming people's emotions can actually shape and form their emotions. She reflects how being called angry 'makes me angry' in a similar way to Grace's noticing that she 'began to feel my body temperature rise and my heart race' when her manager described her as 'anxious'. Lorna also explains how the naming of emotions can shape people's relationships with themselves. For Lorna, a description of her self as 'angry' has a powerful negative effect on her identity so that she feels 'bad' about herself.

Since naming an emotion for one's self or another can move and position people and thereby change relationships between people and with themselves, we might ask what the word is doing in a particular situation and what people prefer or intend to do with the word. Thus we might ask of others, or ourselves, 'What sort of relationship do you want to create here?' Then we could go on to ask, 'And what effect does calling this feeling [admiration] have on your relationship? Does calling this feeling [admiration] help you create the relationship you prefer?' I used these sorts of questions to explore 'anger' with Junior's mother and nurses above. In Chapter 3, I explore the implications of naming emotions for people's identities and propose emotion practices intended to create positive stories of identity with people.

It is not uncommon for people to construct emotions on behalf of others without their participation in the process. Adults often take responsibility for naming children's feelings, as Anya's parents (Chapter 1) identified her 'fear'. Professionals commonly assume the right and duty to name or diagnose emotions on behalf of patients or clients – at the beginning of our work together Sheena asked me to tell her what she was feeling. When people cannot agree a name for an emotion they sometimes turn to a yet

higher authority to resolve their 'feeling dilemma' as when Junior's nurses
appealed to my expertise to pronounce what he was feeling. In situations
like these people often have a notion of the sort of 'core set' of universal
emotions proposed by people like Darwin, with the associated view that it
is possible, with sufficient knowledge, experience or expertise, to accurately
identify and name our own emotions and those of others. However, as we
have seen, appeal to a higher 'emotion authority' does not always offer a
solution to poorly co-ordinated emotion talk. When Grace's manager
named her 'anxiety' she did not accept his authority and felt her 'body temperature rise and her heart race'. It is unlikely Grace and her manager would
have agreed to consult with someone more expert in emotions to help them
resolve the question of what she was feeling. When the nurses attributed
'anger' to Junior A's feeling, he remained silent while his mother appeared
to disengage from the ward team. I have frequently encountered children,
like Junior, who refuse adults' emotion descriptions to explain their behaviour (Fredman, 1997).

Grace's manager and Junior's nurses assumed the right to name their feelings without negotiation. Assuming the authority to identify feelings on
behalf of others implies that people have not only different abilities, but also
different rights and responsibilities, for naming feelings. For example, in my
experience, it is unusual for children to assume the right or be given responsibility to name the feeling of adults. Hence the naming of each other's feelings implies different roles, status or positions of power in the relationship
between those who name and those to whom the name is attributed and
assuming the authority to name another's feeling can position one's self as
knower and the other as less competent. For example, by naming Grace's
emotion on her behalf, her manager asserted his authority as expert, and positioned Grace as less informed or perhaps less competent to name her emotion. On the other hand, by using Jamie's preferred word, 'balup-balup', I
intended to position him as someone who had something meaningful to say
thereby placing responsibility for understanding on myself (Sabat, 2001).

Naming an emotion for oneself or another therefore involves taking a position and thereby positioning the other. The activity of positioning involves
attributing rights and responsibilities, for example my positioning someone
as having something intelligible to say, attributes them the right to our attention and gives me the responsibility to listen and make sense (Davies and
Harré, 1990).

Particular emotion words, according to the cultural contexts that inform
them, will also carry different implications for the way in which they may
position people. For example, a self-description of 'hurt' can imply equal
footing in a relationship (Riikonen and Smith, 1997) or be used as an
appeasement posture (Messent, 2003). On the other hand, describing one-

self as 'angry' often demands the other to be one down and therefore implies moving to a position of more power in relation to another as it does for Lorna in Chapter 3, who describes 'anger', of which she has 'a low opinion', as 'cruel and nasty'.

Thus the naming of emotions is a powerful act that can risk coercion, undermining the other person, colonizing their language or creating an impasse in communication if not negotiated. In the cases of Grace and her manager and of Mrs A, Junior and the ward team, the people involved reached an impasse so they were unable to go on together. Lorna told me she felt bad about herself and angry when others autonomously identified that she was 'angry'. In this chapter, therefore, I offer relational practices towards creating a shared language and common understanding of emotion with each other which include joining the language of the other, adopting an attitude of curiosity and exploring the meanings of emotion words through the contexts of each other's lives. In Chapter 3, I describe further relational practices which involve exploring the stories which inform people's emotion judgements and rules.

CHAPTER 3
Storying emotion

Emotion stories

From 'height phobic' to 'proud hiker'

When I was hiking in the mountains with a friend, my legs began to shake as we negotiated our way down a steep descent. I told myself this was fear recognizing these symptoms as the 'jelly legs' indicative of anxiety, panic or fear described in numerous research papers, clinical reports and textbooks I had read. Never having been partial to heights, I struggled down the rock face in the seated position, miserably anticipating that I was developing a phobia of heights. As we negotiated our return route I noticed my fear developing – I could not look down a ravine we had passed three hours previously.

A year later I reluctantly agreed to hike with my nephew in an area where there were some steep climbs. Engrossed in conversation on the way up I did not notice the steep drop to the ocean. On the way down, I experienced my legs shaking and pointed this out to my nephew who casually reflected, 'You've got shaky legs syndrome'. He proceeded to give me a detailed mechanical explanation that related the 'shaking' to an exertion of pressure to the legs 'common among hikers'. Momentarily I was freed of the 'fear' as I began to pride myself in my 'hiker's legs'.

We could account for my experiences above in several ways with each account telling a different story of the events. A story comprises a sequence of events, actions or states involving actors or characters that are connected by a plot to give meaning to the events. We create stories or narratives to organize our experience, thoughts and feelings into some sort of coherence in order to make sense of our lives, since a narrative offers a way of holding together complex and possibly ambiguous, contradictory or conflicted experiences within a connected pattern of meaning (Bruner, 1990). The use of the word story here does not suggest that

44

people are living a fantasy or that the stories people construct are whimsical. Rather it implies that narratives are constructed to make sense of experience and that the meaning these stories hold provides a framework for interpreting further experiences and for influencing actions.

In the first story I constructed to make sense of my experience on the mountain, I cast myself as the 'height phobic'. The story began with my noticing that my legs were shaking. Interpreting this as a sign of panic, I remembered I had 'never been partial to heights' which consolidated further a story of fear and panic. Thus I went on to extend the sequence of the narrative from my 'fear developing' towards 'anticipating developing a phobia'. This story influenced my future responses to hiking, in particular my diminished enthusiasm for and excessive caution when climbing. In a second story I incorporated my nephew's explanation of 'shaky legs syndrome' which is 'common among hikers' thereby transforming the meanings I gave to my experience of shaky legs from 'fear' to 'physical exertion'. In this narrative, I was able to recall that I 'did not notice the steep drop to the ocean'. A new story in which I cast myself as the 'proud hiker' therefore evolved to replace the story of 'the height phobic', creating the opportunity for me to respond more optimistically to the sensations in my legs. Thus we live our lives according to the stories we tell ourselves and the stories we are told by others. Our stories shape our lives, influencing which experiences we pay attention to, give meaning to and continue to incorporate into our continually evolving narratives (White and Epston, 1990).

Judgements connect with stories

The stories we construct to make sense of our experience reflect our cultural judgements which are an important part of the emotion process. We make judgements about whether it is possible, appropriate or desirable to identify or name an emotion. We ascribe value and meaning to emotions, for example, whether they are positive or negative, desirable or unwanted, suitable or unsuitable. We consider who has the rights and responsibility or perhaps even duty or obligation to name the emotion and we determine whether and how emotions should be shown and expressed. Therefore when exploring emotions with people, I consider what judgement is being expressed by this emotion and since there are always stories connected with the judgements, I invite and listen out for what stories are connected with that emotion.

The judgements we make about our emotions inform rules, often unspoken, that govern our expression of feeling. We continue to form these rules from an early age as we learn to do emotions in our cultures. These rules guide our actions including whether and how we show and perform emotions. Therefore we learn what emotions we can or cannot; should or should not; must or must not; are allowed or not allowed to feel, express, do, think and name.

Everybody must be sad now

> After Tania died, her eight-year-old sister, Miriam, told me that she was 'smiling inside but my face is very sad outside'. When I asked what stopped her smiles from showing outside, she explained to me 'everybody must be sad now so they can see we miss Tania ... so then, how can mama know – I can't keep telling?' (Fredman, 1997)

Miriam shows how we learn through our families and our cultures that certain situations call for particular emotional expression. She has grasped a rule that, in response to her sister's death, she 'must be sad' with her mother and in relation to 'everybody' and 'they', referring to her extended family and their community in Peru. We also learn that certain emotions are permissible within certain relationships and not within others so that we might talk about or even show different emotions in response to the same circumstance dependent on our perception of what is expected, permissible or obligatory in that context. Miriam perceived that it was expected and perhaps obligatory to show sadness with her mother. Weeks later she told me the priest had told her she should be happy that Tania was with God and the angels. Including the priest, God and the angels with her audience, opened opportunities for Miriam to contemplate a wider repertoire of emotional expression.

Contexts informing our stories and judgements

Miriam shows how the stories that inform our emotions are not created in isolation. We construct our emotion stories in relationship with others, present or absent, including our families and communities. Several different contexts might inform the stories we create, the meanings we develop and the actions we take in emotion. As well as the time, place and relationships of the immediate situation, these contexts include the cultures of our ethnicity, family, community, gender, age, religion, profession and sexuality. Miriam learns the sadness rules of her family and culture in relationship with her mother, with reference to the judgements of her community and through the stories of her priest. In Chapter 2, I showed how my stories from different contexts of my life, including the culture of my family of origin, my community and my professional training inform my relationship to jealousy. Later in this chapter, Lorna shares how her family story of violence and abuse has informed her relationship to anger, and Gary relates family, gender and professional stories that inform the rules shaping his relationship to 'unhappiness'.

Gender stories

For Desmond, in Chapter 1, there was no place for feelings at work. As a nurse he had learnt he should 'put your feelings aside and get on with the job'. Thus Desmond was showing a loyalty to the emotion rules of his nurse training and profession. Since emotions have strong gender links (Crawford, Kippax, Onyx, Gault and Benton, 1992), it may be that gender also informed Desmond's relationship to 'feeling'. We acculturate differently as males and females and therefore construct different emotion stories and rules for girls and boys and men and women in many of our cultures. Perhaps Desmond was also participating in a gendered rule that it was not appropriate masculine conduct to discuss feelings at work as Gary shows below.

Feelings are for girls

> Gary sought help with his wife, Liz, because he wanted to 'save' their relationship. Liz was complaining that since Gary had retired from his position as a firefighter he was 'unhappy'. It was not 'Gary's unhappiness' that troubled Liz, but the fact he did not discuss this with her, that he 'shut off', 'never showed his feelings' and 'all I get is his moochy face and silence'. Whereas Liz was not sure whether she wanted to 'stay in this relationship' Gary wanted to 'stay together until death do us part'. When we explored the rules Gary had collected about 'showing feelings' and 'talking about sadness', I learnt that as the oldest son, Gary had taken the message from his father that 'feelings are for the girls, us men get on with the job'. Gary said, ' my sisters were good with feelings – and my little brother, but then he is gay.'

This sort of rule reflects a common cultural story in which emotion, associated with devalued characteristics like irrationality, subjectivity, and chaos, is linked with female whereby women are seen as more emotional than men. In this sort of gendered story, men are often expected to display only certain types of emotion, like anger, if they do become emotional. Women, on the other hand, are expected to display a wider range of emotions with the possible exception of hate and anger, like Gary's sisters who were 'good with feelings'. Also men's emotions are commonly interpreted differently from women's, for example a man's anger is likely to be interpreted as more important, requiring attention, sensible and explicable whereas women's emotions are seen as a natural part of their character or perhaps hormonal (Lutz, 1988).

Therapy stories

Different therapy approaches can be viewed as distinct cultures with their own 'core sets' of emotions, some focusing on anxiety (Freud, 1926), envy (Klein, 1957) or anger (Novaco, 1977) with others concentrating more on stress (Meichenbaum, 1985) or perhaps hope (Frankl, 1963). As emotions do not necessarily show constancy across cultures (Heelas, 1996), practitioners are likely to hold different theories of emotion informed by the various cultures of their preferred therapy approach. We could view these emotion theories as different narratives each informing judgements and rules about emotion display. Hence we might expect practitioners to notice and identify different emotions, attribute different meanings to feelings and differentially evaluate the display of emotions according to the theory that shaped their therapy training and continues to shape their professional development. In turn they are likely to create and act on different rules about whether a particular display of emotion is expected, permissible, obligatory or forbidden within the context of therapy. For example, Mrs. K's social worker below felt obligated to create space for her to 'pour her heart out'.

A jolly good cry

> A social work colleague was concerned he had not been able to find a suitable time to meet with Mrs K, a young mother who was housebound. She was having to care for her four-year-old son who was severely disabled by a life-threatening, progressive neurological disorder and her husband who was bedridden following radical surgery to remove cancer. At their first and only meeting, Mrs K had 'poured her heart out' to the social worker who had intended to visit her regularly to offer her a 'space to have a jolly good cry'. Despite her appreciation and apparent enthusiasm for further meetings, however, Mrs K had not invited the social worker into her home again, always explaining apologetically at the door, that 'the time is not convenient'. The social worker was unsure how he might engage this young mother in a way that might be helpful to her.

When it comes to crying, catharsis has been an influential theory in shaping therapists' practice in the 20th century (Lutz, 1999). Crying has been promoted as beneficial since it is believed that repression and holding in feelings is harmful. A complementary theory proposes that emotions can get stuck in the body when they are not expressed, thereby further inhibiting emotional experience which could lead to depression (Lowen, 1975). People informed by these theories usually believe they should enable people to 'let out' and 'be in touch' with their feelings. I have encountered many practitioners, like the social worker above, who use versions of this theory to inform their therapeutic role as primarily to help people express emotion. The social worker held something of a hydraulic theory of emotions, believing that crying could help Mrs K 'express her repressed emotions' which could enable her to 'work through the loss of the healthy family she was mourning'. Thus he felt obligated to 'give her space to tell her story and have a jolly good cry'.

I wondered with the social worker what story Mrs K would tell of their meeting and whether she shared his theory of crying. I was curious that she had not welcomed further offers of his 'crying therapy'. I began to reflect on theories that question the usefulness of tears and that challenge the view that crying helps us get in touch with pain. For example, Freud (1896) himself eventually abandoned cathartic therapy on the basis that crying could have no therapeutic value in and of itself without bringing the experience into words. Also there is the idea that crying allows us to turn away from, rather than get in touch with, the cause of our pain in that tears redirect our emotions, shifting our attention from our thoughts to our bodies. By turning inward and toward our own bodily sensations, our own feelings, we are able to divert our attention from the source of our pain (Lutz, 1999). I shared some of these alternative theories about crying, not as better or more correct theses but as alternative narratives, with the social worker who became curious about the idea that we store 'frustrated desires' rather than 'frustrated emotions' (Freud, 1900). As he began to think of Mrs K's tears as signals of her desire and therefore indicative of hope, he began to wonder what she wished for.

> On the phone to Mrs K, the social worker reflected that he had been think-ing for some time about the strength and courage she had been showing through this difficult time. He invited her to talk with him about ways he could support her strength and courage so that she could get the most out of it. He expressed interest in what she would like now and in the future for her family and herself. As usual, Mrs K said she would very much like to see the social worker. The next time he visited, she welcomed him in – she had baked a cake in preparation for his visit.

Without talking to Mrs K we cannot know whether she perceived an unwanted moral obligation to cry with the social worker, whether she felt better or worse after her initial weeping meeting with him or whether there were other explanations for her repeated refusals to meet. However we can know that, when the social worker's intention shifted from help-ing Mrs K to 'have a jolly good cry' and 'get it all out' to inviting her to explore her desires and hopes, 'what she would like for now and the future', she welcomed him into her home.

In the same way that therapists have diverse theories about clients' crying, so they tell multiple stories about laughing which inform the judge-ments they make about when, whether or how people laugh in the process of therapy. Whereas numerous people have complained to me about the 'pressure to cry' in sessions with professionals, I have never met a client who has described a pressure to laugh. In fact, if anything, clients have reported the opposite. For example, when I was training as a psychotherapist, a father who had been seen with his family by several different professionals in that centre made a joke which I did not understand in our first meeting. In response to my intended 'neutral' reaction, he told his family 'they don't laugh at this centre'. Although it had never been formally stated, this father had taken away the rule that laughter was not expected or perhaps permissible in the centre. Perhaps he had picked up on a commonly held belief that laughter was inappropriate during therapy.

Theories about laughter include accounts of its healing properties, for example increased relaxation following a reduction in muscle tension, lowered blood pressure and enhanced digestion. Laughter has also been promoted as an anaesthetic for pain, a release for stress and tension and as treatment for a range of physical conditions (Lemma, 2000). However, it is unusual, in my experience, to find therapists who openly report, and especially promote, laughter in therapy. When I have explored the rules guiding therapists' approach to laughter in workshops or supervision sessions, I have encountered many therapists who believe laughter should not be encouraged in therapy and relate stories about laughter 'masking real feelings' or being used as a 'manic defence' like my colleague below.

What has she got to laugh about?

A psychologist colleague expressed concern that her client, Ellen, had been 'laughing inappropriately for two sessions now'.

Glenda: How do you know her laughter is inappropriate?

Colleague: She's dying for God's sake. What has she got to laugh about? I know I shouldn't let this go on for much longer but short of ... phwah [she made a vigorous punching gesture with her fist] ... I really don't know what to do.

Glenda: Phwah? [copying my colleague's gesture]

Colleague: I mean pushing her to get in touch with – facing her death, the end. But it seems so violent – that's what I mean it would be ...

Glenda: Mmm tricky ... You know I'm thinking, what do you think would happen ... uh what's the risk of following her laughter – sort of being with her in her laughter? I don't know – finding out where it takes Ellen? [Noticing my colleague frowning] Does that sound a bit weird?

Colleague: No. I'm just worried I'd be colluding.

I went on to share with my colleague an idea that I have come across that laughter can enable family and friends to stay close and supportive in the face of distress or fear which might overwhelm or create distance (Lemma, 2000). This idea reminded my colleague that Ellen 'was a breath of fresh air' on the ward, 'the nurses can't keep away from her'. Together we used the idea to think more about why Ellen might want to keep my colleague engaged with her, what conversations she might want to have and whether she would want to talk about her dying or her death, her life or her living. We continue this conversation between Ellen and the psychologist in Chapter 5.

The stories therapists tell about the expression of anger in therapy are also diverse.

Room for anger

> Sue, a clinical psychologist, consulted me for help with her relationship with her client. Kevin had had to end psychoanalytic therapy with his male psychotherapist whom he had been seeing three days a week for the past 10 months because he could no longer afford to pay the fees. Therefore he had been referred to a public health service psychology department where he had seen Sue for three of his contracted 10 sessions of cognitive behavioural therapy. Sue said Kevin had shouted and sworn at each therapy session, complaining constantly of feeling angry. She was 'uncomfortable with him in the room' because 'that show of aggression in a 45-year-old man frightened' her so she was unsure whether she could continue to work with him.
>
> I invited Sue to reflect on the 'emotion culture' that might have been created between Kevin and his previous therapist. For example, I wondered what stories had been told about the expression of feelings in therapy, in particular anger, how a display of this sort of 'anger' was judged within this first psychotherapy relationship and what rules were connected. Interested to explore these questions with Kevin, Sue learnt that Kevin had been encouraged to 'acknowledge his anger' during his previous therapy. Sue went on to let Kevin know he had convinced her he was well able to acknowledge and even to express his anger in their sessions. She suggested he was 'now ready to progress to the next step' and therefore invited him to 'constructively channel his anger' in their final six sessions. According to Sue, Kevin embraced his final sessions of therapy with enthusiasm. At each session he answered questions thoughtfully, recorded his thoughts, feelings and behaviour between sessions and successfully negotiated different strategies and ways of thinking that helped him gain confidence to challenge his difficulties. Kevin completed his 10-session contract with Sue without a further episode of anger.

It may be that Kevin's abilities to 'acknowledge' and express anger were shaped within the culture of his previous psychotherapy in which anger was accepted or perhaps even expected. This culture would have been created in the relationship between Kevin and his therapist and also informed by the ideas about anger and emotions which both Kevin and his therapist brought to their therapeutic relationship from other contexts of their lives. For example, we might wonder how the gendered stories about anger of these two men might have informed and shaped their joint relationship to anger. We might also wonder what the psychotherapist's professional stories about anger were and how they informed the emotion talk in the sessions. When Sue joined Kevin in a new therapy contract, they created a different culture of emotion between them in which anger was not expected or perhaps not permissible. Sue, a woman and clinical psychologist working within a therapeutic orientation of cognitive behavioural therapy, was most likely informed by different gender and professional rules about the expression of anger in a therapy session from the rules informing Kevin's former male, psychoanalytic psychotherapist. Thus we cannot make sense of Kevin's expression as 'anger' or 'aggression' through only his actions of shouting and swearing or through only Sue's reactions of discomfort and fear. Rather the meaning of this emotion is located in their 'joint action' (Shotter, 1984) or how they co-ordinate (Pearce, 1989) their actions.

Each therapeutic approach has not only rules for how and whether clients express emotion but also therapists have clear rules about the propriety of displaying emotion themselves in the professional context. In a supervision session with me, Julia, a counsellor who had been deeply moved by a client's experience, began to cry and then apologized for her crying.

> *Julia:* [tearfully] I'm sorry … I'm sorry. I feel so stupid for crying. That's why I can't think – I feel guilty for taking your time.
>
> *Glenda:* Guilty? Stupid? I don't understand. Why guilty and why stupid?
>
> *Julia:* I don't know. I shouldn't be crying. It's not professional.
>
> *Glenda:* Professional? Do you have that rule for all professionals?
>
> *Julia:* No – I don't judge others.
>
> *Glenda:* Is it OK for others – even professionals to cry?
>
> *Julia:* Yes.
>
> *Glenda:* So you have a different rule for yourself – when it comes to crying?
>
> *Julia:* I guess I'm quite hard on myself.
>
> *Glenda:* So where do these different rules you are using for yourself – where do they come from?

Like Julia, many of the counsellors and therapists attending my workshops on emotions have rules that prescribe or proscribe the show of feelings in the professional context. For many, laughing or crying in front of clients and patients is a particular taboo. Therapists might hold positive cultural beliefs about crying from their own families or gender, for example, that tears are a sign of tribute or devotion, a mark of sincerity, an indication of hope or a reflection of empathy. They also might view crying positively for clients yet proscribe crying for themselves with a client in the context of a therapeutic relationship. There is a widely shared belief among practitioners that in a professional context, tears reflect that feeling has overcome thinking and interfered with the professional's ability to speak or help the client. To cry in a professional relationship, therefore, is to 'break down' or to be over-whelmed with tears. To laugh within a professional therapeutic relationship on the other hand, has been described as making light of the situation or showing disrespect. As one counsellor told me, 'I would like to be myself with clients ... I think I must come across as so stiff in the therapy context ... but I have learnt that a good professional remains detached'.

In Chapter 5, I discuss how therapists and counsellors might extend the repertoire of emotion stories and postures they might take into therapeutic conversations.

Stories of identity

Emotion stories are intricately connected not only to our relationships with our families, communities and cultures but also to our relationship with our selves. The stories we tell of emotions express judgements that are commonly linked with definitions of identity and therefore have different implications for how we perceive the moral worth of our selves and others. Thus our identities are created in emotion stories that talk to us of our abilities, who we were, who we are and who we can become. Describing and acknowledging our emotions can therefore enhance or diminish our experiences of our selves. Above, Julia discusses how she constructs a negative identity of her self, in particular her professional self, when she cries in a supervision session. Julia connects crying to stories of unprofessional behaviour. In Chapter 2, Lorna showed me how attributing emotion terms, if unwanted and deemed unsuitable, can create negative identities for the people being named. She shared her judgement that anger is negative and undesirable, 'Nobody likes to be seen as angry ... would you?' and that she 'ends up feeling bad about feeling angry'.

I have noticed that emotion names are most commonly refused when the naming connects to a story that undermines a person's sense of wor-thiness or autonomy or when unilateral ascription of a feeling by others suggests his or her own incompetence. Junior A's pointed ignoring of the nurses' naming of his anger in Chapter 2 suggested his refusal of that self description and led me to consider that he may have perceived 'angry' as a negative evaluation of his self. Grace's response suggests she did not view her manager's description of her 'anxiety' as a positive statement about her competence.

Exploring stories and judgements through the contexts of people's lives

Above, I have discussed how, as therapists and clients, we bring a repertoire of judgements about the expression of emotions to the therapeutic relationship. These judgements are informed by different stories from our personal and professional cultures and inform the rules that guide how and whether we show emotion. In this way we learn both restraint in expression and the conventions of emotional expression.

The rules and judgements people make about emotion are unique to their contexts and to their relationships with self and others. To know how to go on with people in emotion therefore requires an understanding of the contexts of their emotion – what judgements they make, what stories inform those judgements, and what rules guide their actions. Therefore, I explore, with curiosity, the moral orders of people's emotion through the different contexts of their lives, listening for the judgements they are making about expression of their feeling and the rules informing their display.

To bring forth the stories connected with emotions I pay attention to the judgements people are making, listening for words like 'must/must not', 'should/should not', 'can/cannot' as moral indicators of what people believe is obligatory, forbidden, expected and permissible. I then go on to explore the contexts of their judgements with questions like 'Where does that [judgement or idea] come from?' or 'Whose voices do you hear [telling that rule]? What do they say?' which can open space for a story to be told. Questions like 'When might you view [this emotion] in a different way?' or 'Is there anyone in your community who has a different view?' can elicit further stories from different contexts informing the emotion.

Below I become curious about the stories informing Lorna's judgement of anger. She had just told me that one could always tell when a person is angry because 'it's on your face'.

> *Glenda:* So are you saying you don't like to show anger – have people see it on your face?
>
> *Lorna:* Mmm I don't want people to see.
>
> *Glenda:* How come? What do you think about anger? How do you see it?
>
> *Lorna:* I have a very low opinion of it.
>
> *Glenda:* Very low – uh what is your low opinion of anger? Can you tell me more to help me understand?
>
> *Lorna:* It's cruel and nasty.
>
> *Glenda:* Ah? Where does that come from? That it's cruel and nasty? Did someone tell you or something like that?
>
> *Lorna:* They showed me.

Glenda: Showed you? How? Who showed you? Is this OK to talk about here Lorna? Today?

Lorna: I don't mind. My mother and my brothers – they were, all of them, an angry lot. My father treated them bad, I know. But look where it got them.

Glenda: Did they show their anger?

Lorna: Oh yes. My mother too. She lost it.

Glenda: Lost control?

Lorna: [nods]

In the course of our conversation the story informing Lorna's perspectives on anger emerges. I learn that her father had left her family soon after she was born, that her mother and brothers were 'always angry' and they 'took it out on' Lorna. They showed their anger through violence so Lorna received frequent beatings from her mother and described herself as 'tormented' by her brothers. She also related how her mother's 'twisty face' used to frighten her.

Lorna relates her family stories of aggression that include cruelty, violence and lack of control. These stories inform her judgement of anger as 'cruel and nasty' and perhaps uncontrollable, and seem to have influenced her decision towards not showing anger. She refuses to participate in any ongoing narrative with people about *her* 'anger' which she says leaves her feeling 'bad' about herself since 'nobody likes to be seen as angry'. Lorna cannot think of a single instance when anger might be justified. In this sense her family stories of anger exert a strong contextual force on how she acts (Cronen, Johnson and Lannaman, 1982), constraining her expression of anger in any situation.

For Gary, above, however, the situation is not so straightforward. He holds a number of different and potentially contradictory rules about showing feelings. It is not always clear to Gary what rule to follow.

For their relationship to continue Liz wanted Gary to 'share his unhappiness', with her. Gary said he was willing to do anything to 'save' their relationship and agreed to pursue Liz's suggestion that he see me on his own to help him 'get in touch with his feelings'.

I asked Liz and Gary to help me understand more of where they were coming from with regards to 'sharing unhappiness' so that I might get a better sense of how best to approach feelings in our conversations. I was interested in their judgements associated with 'unhappiness' and their cultural stories connected with their judgements about discussing or showing feelings. I wanted to understand what rules from their cultures might be informing how and whether they believed they could or should show unhappiness. How were people expected to perform 'unhappiness' in the cultures of their families, genders, sexuality, and careers and in the context of their relationship with each other? Therefore I invited Gary and Liz to explore the stories and judgements connected with 'unhappiness' through the different contexts of their lives. I asked questions that explored how their different contexts informed how they performed and related to emotions. For example 'How do you do unhappiness in your family?', 'Is it expected that a woman/man in your culture would show [this emotion] in this situation?', 'What is your religious view of [this emotion]?', 'How would a gay man of your age show sadness?'

Gary described himself as 'useless at feelings but good in a crisis' and recounted several stories in which this very combination had served him well in his successful career as a firefighter where there was no time for feelings at work. According to Gary, a competent firefighter should be good in a crisis and cannot take time for feelings. This rule fitted with the emotion training he received in his family, in particular from his father, that 'feelings are for the girls and men get on with the job'. That his 'sisters were good with feelings' fitted well with Gary's gendered and family judgements and rules about the expression of feelings. He accounted for his youngest 'little' brother's ability with feelings in terms of his sexuality 'but then he is gay'. Constructing gay men as a different category of man seemed to enable Gary to create different emotion rules for gay men from heterosexual men. In this way he was able to acknowledge his brother's ability with feelings and avoid contradicting his own rule that 'competent men should not show emotion' thereby maintaining a coherence with the rules of his gender, family, career and sexuality.

In our conversations with Liz, however, it became apparent that the idea that 'feelings are for girls and men should get on with the job' was not coherent with what was required for Gary to be a 'good husband' to Liz or to 'save' their relationship. Therefore the rule that he should avoid emotion talk or the expression or acknowledgement of emotion did not fit with the rules he and Liz were creating in the context of their relationship. What we see here is a contradiction or conflict between some of his emotion rules that create something of a bind for Gary. Getting on with the job, being good in a crisis and not focusing on feelings would confirm his view of himself as a competent man. These actions were consistent with a version of manhood Gary had constructed through the contexts of his family of origin, his relationship with his father and his work as a firefighter. However not discussing his feelings would challenge his ability to save his relationship with Liz. To be a good husband to Liz, he would need to express his 'unhappiness' and discuss his feelings, which would however challenge his view of himself as a competent man.

Although Gary was willing to meet with me on his own to 'learn how to express his feelings', I raised the dilemma he might face with respect to his view of himself as a competent man if we were successful in this task. We were able to name this dilemma in the form of questions: 'How could Gary save his marriage and still feel good about himself as a man?'; 'How could he be a competent man and a good husband?'; 'How could sharing unhappiness enable him to be a good husband and a competent man?' Gary said I had 'put [my] finger right on it', he had been feeling 'less of a man' since leaving the fire service. Thus we can see how Gary's identity, his view of himself as a man and a husband, are intricately connected to his many layered stories, judgements and rules about showing feelings, especially 'unhappiness'.

Exploring implications of emotion for identity

In therapy I try to participate in descriptions of people's emotions that create life-enhancing stories of identity rather than descriptions that create life-diminishing stories of identity (Lang, 1999). Therefore, when I engage in emotion talk I am curious about the effects of different emotion descriptions on people's stories of identity. I am interested in their preferred identities – what stories they want told about their selves, what abilities they want recognized – and how different emotion descriptions enable or constrain their preferred versions of self. Therefore I begin by exploring how the emotion description fits with their preferred story of self and whether it enhances or diminishes the abilities they want recognized.

When Lorna told me 'nobody likes to be seen as angry', I assumed she did not perceive 'anger' as a positive ability and that she did not want people to tell a story of herself as 'angry'. I checked my assumption by asking her, 'How would you like to be seen?', 'How would you like people to talk about you?' and went on to explore how a description of 'angry' enabled or constrained how she preferred to see herself with questions like:

– If you choose to describe yourself as angry how does that affect how you see your self?
– Do you like your self more or less? What opportunities does this provide?

These sorts of questions also helped me to explore the meanings and effects of acknowledging 'anger' on Christine B's view of self.

I hate myself

Christine B had undergone surgery, chemotherapy and radiotherapy for a brain tumour that was originally identified when she was nine years old. She had been in good health for five years until a regrowth of the tumour had required further treatment. At our weekly meeting, Christine, now 15

complained of 'hating myself'. I learnt she had spent the past three days
'feeling angry' towards several of her school friends who had teased her
about her 'baldness' when she had returned to school after her first bout
of surgery and chemotherapy, age nine. What was troubling Christine most
was her 'anger' which involved 'thinking up nasty things to say to them'
and sometimes 'wishing they would lose all their hair so they can know
what it feels like'. When I clarified, 'what kind of anger would you call this?
Is it a good anger or not so good?' Christine was adamant that all anger
was 'a sin' since 'if you're a good Christian you don't feel angry' and
confirmed she wanted to be a good Christian.

Christine named her own feeling as anger and this description gave meaning to her experiences of resentment in relation to her friends who teased
her. However, informed by her stories of her religion, she negatively evaluated this anger. Thus the 'angry Christine' narrative evolved to inform a
negative identity story of Christine as a bad person who was sinful and
evil. In this sense, Christine's story of anger did not fit with her preferred
story of herself as a good Christian.

When people's cultural or religious stories inform negative stories of self
as they did with Christine above, I find myself facing an ethical dilemma.
My intention is to work towards self-enhancing rather than self-diminishing stories with people. I also intend to respect people's preferred cultural
narratives. Thus with Christine I was unclear how I could go on. If I joined
her in her story, I could be confirming that she was 'sinful' and 'bad'. However, if I disagreed with her views, I would be undermining her religious
beliefs and negating the same story that had helped her through some of
the most difficult parts of her treatments.

In situations like these, I do not challenge people's preferred stories.
Instead I try to participate in the co-creation of stories that are different from the presenting narrative. That is, I participate in the construction of alternative stories, offering different ways of evaluating the
emotion, with a view to opening space for the creation of new meanings and hence new and preferred views of self as well as new possibilities
for action.

Opening space for new stories and new possibilities

Inviting alternative stories

My intention is to invite people to identify a range of emotion stories, perhaps previously untold, from the different contexts of their lives with a
view to opening space for new meanings for the emotion and alternative
ways to go on. For example, addressing the context of religion I might

ask, 'What does your priest/rabbi/imam say about this?', or connecting with the context of gender I might enquire, 'If you were a man/woman, what ideas would you have?' Often I propose that we invite other significant people, such as members of the family, culture or community to share their perspectives in order to elaborate further our repertoire of possible emotion stories.

For example, I asked Christine if there was anyone we could speak with who could help me understand more about Christian views on anger. She recommended her mother and although we usually met on our own, she agreed to her joining for part of our next meeting.

> After we had explained to Mrs B how 'anger' had been leading Christine into periods of self-hatred, I asked her, 'Could you help us here? Christine tells me feeling anger is a sin. She says she hates herself when she feels angry. She wants to continue to be a good Christian. I do not know a lot about Christianity, I thought maybe you could tell us – are there times, as a good Christian, when you might see anger as justified – as not a sin but OK in the circumstance? Are there any examples of this that you know? What would Christ have to say on the matter? Have you any idea?' Mrs B responded immediately, speaking directly to Christine, 'Of course, when Christ turned over the tables.' I was not familiar with this story so Mrs B and Christine told me how Christ had found people engaged in moneylending in the temple and in anger 'turned over the tables'.

I have found that juxtaposing different theses in this way can be especially useful when people's narratives, like Christine's, bring forth disapproving views of self.

Inviting alternatives, exceptions or even opposites and contradictions can make it possible for people to make new connections and associations between their story and the alternative story, thereby creating opportunities for syntheses that might offer new meanings and alternative options for action. Initially Christine's privileged story about anger informed by her Christian belief that 'anger is a sin', brought forth a negative view of herself as a bad person. When her mother was invited to identify a thesis different from Christine's 'sinful' narrative, she shared a story in which anger was justified when used to communicate appropriate displeasure or invite more morally acceptable behaviour. The juxtaposing of this new story with Christine's story, created opportunities for Christine, her mother and I to talk about different sorts of anger and the situations in which it might be acceptable or perhaps even appropriate to feel or show anger.

Mrs B's story about Christ reminded me of another story I had been told as a child in which Moses had broken the golden calf in anger when people were worshipping idols. After sharing this story with Christine and

Mrs B, we went on to reflect on Christ's position, Moses's circumstances and Christine's circumstances in relation to anger.

> Quite spontaneously Christine suggested, 'Jesus would have agreed with Moses' so her mother and I joined her in imagining how a conversation between them might have progressed. An idea emerged that anger can be useful and justified 'when used sparingly' (Mrs B's words) to communicate or get people to respond when 'simple talk' is not being heard. Hence we began to think about what Christine would like to communicate to whom and what sorts of talk or actions would enable her to be heard. Thus a different story from the 'anger is sinful' story emerged in which Christine spoke of the unfairness of her illness and the cruel treatment she received from school friends. She thought her priest would agree with the view that, 'used sparingly anger was justified to get people to notice when they are doing wrong' but wanted to 'check him out' to make sure. She said she was 'not bothered' to tell her friends about the hurt they had inflicted on her in the past, but felt she would 'feel allowed to confront them if they go wrong again'.

Although anger did not emerge as an issue in further sessions with Christine, I have added the stories of anger we generated in our conversation to a repertoire of stories about anger I continue to develop and share with people in supervision and therapeutic conversations.

Introducing alternative stories

Christine and her mother generated a rich collection of emotion stories from the multiple contexts of their lives. There are times, however, when asking questions does not invite emotion stories since people have 'never had the chance', 'never been allowed', 'never felt safe enough' or 'never chosen' to talk about or perform the emotion. Others have said, 'I know what I think but I want to hear what you think.' Even when people do generate many stories of the emotion from the different contexts of their lives, their stories may be so coherent with each other that they all reflect the same rules or messages and therefore again offer few new perspectives or different possibilities. For example, Lorna related several family stories of anger all carrying versions of the message that anger was 'cruel and nasty' and all justifying or obligating an outright injunction against anger for Lorna. Therefore, if we have not been able to generate a useful repertoire of emotion stories to inform new possibilities or if people specifically invite my 'professional opinion', as Gavin does in Chapter 7, I may offer stories or theories of emotions to clients. I offer the stories tentatively and speculatively not as truths but as further possibilities in the way that I contributed one of my cultural stories into the pool of narratives Christine and her mother were generating about anger.

I present the different stories and theories of emotions to clients as offerings, not as truths within an implicit hierarchy of knowledges, but as possible stories that take their place among other theses – cultural, religious, communal and professional. I try to put these theories forward as more or less useful ideas that might contribute to the creation of the client's preferred story of the emotion. Instead of identifying any particular theory as the best or right way to think, therefore, I invite clients to evaluate how the different stories fit with their own personal and professional contexts. Therefore I may pause to consider with clients the possible uses of a particular theory and the opportunities or constraints it might present them. For example, when Lorna asked me, 'Would you like to be seen as angry? [Laughing] You said you would answer my question', I shared the theories that emotions are communicative (Oatley and Johnson-Laird, 1996) and function to alter our interactions (Oatley, 1996) thereby adjusting the terms of our relationships (Averill, 1982).

> *Glenda:* I thought that was a really good question actually. It made me think – why would I want people to notice I am angry. Well – sometimes I might want to use anger – like shouting, or showing it on my face so people can see it – to sort of move people – to get them to change towards me or to notice ...
>
> *Lorna:* [Interrupting] That's what I was saying – my mum, my brothers ... They did – but I don't –
>
> *Glenda:* Are you saying that you have chosen not to show anger?
>
> Lorna [nods]
>
> *Glenda:* What have you done instead – I mean to get people to notice, or when you are wanting to change things between you and say ...
>
> *Lorna:* These days I speak really loud and clear – the MS has taught me that.
>
> *Glenda:* Loud and clear. And that works for you – I see. So what do you think of this idea then that we might show anger to try to change things between ourselves and others? Do you think it could be useful to you at some time?
>
> *Lorna:* Not a lot [laughs]. It doesn't do much for me.

Like Lorna, Anthony, who meets with me in supervision, did not find the ideas of 'anger as communication' or 'showing anger to adjust relationships' a good fit.

> Anthony told me that he 'had to show I was angry' to his boss who, he believed, had 'humiliated' a member of his team in front of other colleagues. When I asked what he was hoping his anger would communicate and what effect he wanted to have on his boss, Anthony corrected me, 'I'm not trying

to get him to hear anything, I've given that up a long time ago. I know it won't achieve anything. This is for my integrity. I have to confront him. I can't just sit there and watch what he does. I am the sort of person who stands up for people's rights.'

Anthony's moral obligation to show anger in order to maintain his 'integrity' resonates for me with another theory which says that anger relates to a 'demeaning offence' against our selves and who or what is important to us (Lazarus, 1991). Hence anger is a demand or invitation for some sort of retribution or recompense for this perceived transgression (Riikonen and Smith, 1997). I offered this idea about anger to Lorna.

Glenda: Your question about why I would want people to notice I am angry, I was thinking of something I read – that sometimes we experience anger, we feel anger in situations of injustice – like when we feel we have been humiliated or put down or someone has discriminated against us or …

Lorna: [nodding]

Glenda: So I was thinking – I think that's when I would want people to notice – or maybe that's what I want people to notice – that something is not fair, or they are being unjust or I am being discrim…

Lorna: [nodding, interrupting] Discriminated mmm … I feel discriminated you know – I know you know, like Judith Cross.

[In a previous meeting Lorna had been sharing her frustrations of living with disability with me. I had told her about a paper I had read in which Judith Cross (1990) had openly discussed her own experience of disability. I had given this paper to Lorna at her request.]

Glenda: Mm uhm …

Lorna: It's not anger – discriminated is more right

Glenda: Mmm … Is it something to do with …

Lorna: Yes … discriminated … people judge you.

Lorna named her feeling as 'discriminated' not 'anger'. We continued to have a conversation about discrimination and injustice. Moving away from a focus on 'anger' we both became interested in the effects of discrimination on people's dignity and what she and others could do to recognize and respect her dignity. Neither Lorna nor Anthony found the stories that 'we use anger to move others' and that 'ventilation of anger releases stress' useful. If I were guided by those stories I would most likely have contemplated, 'How can I get them to express their anger?' Informed by the story that 'people express anger to restore dignity' which seemed to fit better for both Lorna and Anthony, we were able to consider instead, 'What is the dignity that needs to be restored?' and 'What moral order do we need to connect with?'

Usually I verbally relate professional theories to people, although there have been times when I have shared written material. I have noticed that each time I relate a theory, it evolves in different ways, modifying in relationship with the audience. Therefore, the theories I describe to Lorna above are not presented as accurate representations of the original theories. Instead they are versions of some of the professional theories I have gleaned over time and have then co-evolved with the people in our conversations. In Chapter 7, I present versions of these same theories to Gavin towards co-creating quite different emotion stories.

As we live our lives we experience physical sensations and we act, interact and create stories about these experiences. Emotion is the story we weave of our sensations, displays and judgements through the multi-layered contexts of our lives. That is we create the emotion story in relationships with others, present and absent and with reference to memories and stories of our cultures. When the storyline changes, therefore, the emotion changes. In this chapter I describe exploring the emotion stories people construct through the different contexts of their lives. This approach begins to loosen or deconstruct the emotion stories, opening space for different feelings and actions. I also propose further relational practices to change the storyline, for example, inviting alternative stories and introducing new stories to the client. Having addressed how emotion stories are intricately woven with stories of identity, I reflect on how we might co-create stories that enhance rather than diminish people's identities. In Chapter 4, I introduce the body into the story, not as the container of emotion but as a medium for communication and relationship.

CHAPTER 4
Understanding emotion

Knowing what you feel

> Kathy came to see me on her 26th birthday, three weeks after the death of her mother. When I asked how she wanted to use our time together, she replied, 'I think you should know what happened – so you can know how I am feeling' and went on to relate some details of the circumstances of her mother's death by suicide.

At the time I did not clarify with Kathy how her telling me 'what happened' might help me 'know' her feelings. I assumed she expected I could deduce her feelings from knowledge of the facts she reported of her experience and from my professional theories of people's responses to suicide. This sort of understanding implies what John Shotter (1993) refers to as a rational sort of knowing. To have a rational knowing of what Kathy was feeling would involve 'knowing what' happened and 'knowing that' people in this sort of situation are likely to respond in a particular way. Thus rational knowing involves a theoretical or descriptive sort of knowledge and the idea that we take in new facts, clarify information or hold understanding in our heads, and then use the information to inform what we do.

When Kathy mentioned her mother had 'killed herself', I did wonder to myself whether I had sufficient knowledge of suicide to be helpful to her. For a moment I regretted I had not attended a course that lays out the 'dos and don'ts' of responding to people bereaved by suicide. At this point I was aspiring to a 'rational knowing' by assuming that meta-theories, for example bereavement theories or research on suicide, could help me know what Kathy might be feeling or even what she might go on to feel in the future. I was also looking to a 'practical knowing' whereby a suitable repertoire of methods, skills and rules might guide my responses.

Throughout her telling, Kathy sobbed, gulping air and words together as she spoke, so that her speech came in fits and starts. I kept checking, 'Is this OK to go on … telling me like this?' Her sobbing and her story moved me to the edge of tears myself. I swallowed hard and felt a pricking sensation in my eyes. Struggling to find the words to connect to her experience, I drifted between what Tom Andersen (1992) might call 'inner and outer talks', mostly 'inner talks' as I asked myself, 'What should I do here now? Is it OK to just sit and be with her now?'

I wanted to know how to be with Kathy in this moment and found referring to theories, ideas and practice guidelines did not help me understand how to respond. Participating within the conversation with her, I was affected by what we were creating between us and wanted to know 'what should I do?' A consideration of 'what do I know?' did not help me know how to go on, but positioned me instead as if I was 'outside' of and unaffected by the conversation in which we were engaged. Thus it was not a rational or practical knowing that could enable me to be with Kathy, but a knowing of a third kind (Shotter, 1993), a relational knowing that involves knowing how to relate to our situation. Relational knowing emphasizes not a 'knowing that' or a 'knowing what', as in knowing what bereavement theories and suicide research might say that Kathy would be feeling. Rather it highlights a 'knowing from' the contexts of the other as well as knowing from our own contexts, as in knowing from what Kathy has shown and told me and knowing from my own experience with Kathy.

In the beginning of our talking I felt awkward and clumsy in response to Kathy. In my private talks I repeatedly reflected, 'Is it OK to simply sit and be with her now?'; 'I am really not being of any help'; 'That comment I just made was so inept – a platitude'; 'I cannot find the words to connect respectfully with her experience'; 'If I say nothing will she feel lonely in her despair?'; 'Is she wanting me to be with her in this experience so she can show me how she feels?'

Kathy's tears and words touched and moved me. As I sat with her and listened I was able to attend to how I was affected in the moment and to my private talk. I tried to use this knowing from my own experience with Kathy to help me learn further from her by sharing the thoughts and feelings I was having in the form of questions. Thus I used my repeated thoughts, 'Is it OK to simply sit and be with her now?' and 'Is she wanting me to be with her in this experience so that she can show me how she feels?' to guide my talking with Kathy. Therefore I asked, 'Is it OK to be with you like this, Kathy, if I sit and listen quietly while you tell me?'

Creating responsive understanding

Relational knowing is a joint knowing that we need in order to go on with other people. Understanding Kathy therefore did not involve a purely mental process on my part, but our joint ability to co-ordinate in talk and in action so we could know how to go on. Creating this sort of shared understanding involves not a one-shot achievement, but a back-and-forth process of negotiating between the people participating in the conversation. Rather than a process of passing ideas, thoughts or feelings from one person's body through language to another, it involves a gradual to-and-fro process of responding to each other, testing and checking with each other in the course of a conversation. In this sense we are acting in a 'sensuous responsive' way (Shotter, 1993).

> Since Kathy told me it was 'fine' for me to sit and listen quietly while she related her experience, we sat together for a while, Kathy talking some of the time, sometimes weeping quietly, sometimes sobbing. No longer preoccupied by whether I could 'simply sit with Kathy' or critical of my own 'inept' responses, I was able to move to other reflections. I began to think about my own mother's death, which filled me with dread so that I wanted to distance from Kathy's experience. I tried to imagine what I would want from someone like me in that moment and again returned to the question, 'What shall I do or say?'

I went on to use our experience-in-common to further inform my talking with Kathy.

> *Glenda:* I have been really touched by what you have told me. And now I am wondering whether what I am feeling and thinking – being here with you – is connected in any way to what you have been going through at all. Would you be interested to hear and tell me if my experience is familiar to you in any way? Maybe it is not.
>
> *Kathy:* Yeah ... go on then.
>
> *Glenda:* As you spoke I was saying to myself, 'What should I do here now? I'm really not being of any help.' I was also thinking, 'That comment I made was so inept' and 'If I say nothing will she feel lonely?'
>
> *Kathy:* [nodding and crying softly]
>
> *Glenda:* 'Feeling inept' or 'feeling of no help' – do they connect with you – are they familiar to anything you have been going through lately? I was just wondering ...?
>
> *Kathy:* That's how I felt with my mother, all the time. I should have done more for her. She was lonely – I couldn't find anything to help her see life in a positive way.

Through a back-and-forth process of negotiating, checking and testing, Kathy and I began to create joint understanding. Touched by her words and actions and contemplating our experience-in-common, I reflected something of my experience of being with her and invited Kathy to tell me if she resonated with any of my reflections. I was hoping that her response could help me learn from her how to be with her in the moment and how to make sense of her experience in the ways she would like me to understand. Kathy's telling took me beyond a rational knowing of merely the facts of what happened. Through being with her as she related her story, I was touched by her words and moved by her actions towards something of a sense of what she had been through, of what the experience was like for her and of how we could be together through this. Exploring Kathy's feeling in this way led to more of what John Shotter (Shotter and Katz, 1996) might call my responsive understanding than a rational, representational or referential understanding. In retrospect I am wondering whether Kathy's suggestion – 'I think you should know what happened – so you can know how I am feeling' – could have been her invitation to me to participate in creating understanding through being with her in the process of her telling and my listening to her experience. Therefore, perhaps she was intending to present her experience rather than, as I initially assumed, to represent it.

Above we can note the back-and-forth process of negotiating, testing and checking between Kathy and I that is involved in creating understanding between people. I began by focusing on my responses to Kathy's actions in the moment and was asking questions rather than asserting assumptions. Hence I was offering my theories and experiences as invitations to explore further understandings rather than as fact or truth.

Knowing from our bodies

We could say that my understanding of Kathy's feelings began not in my mind but in the activity of my body. (James Griffith and Melissa Elliot point out that our mind is in our bodies). As she told her story, and I sat with her in her weeping, the most powerful information I received was initially through my body. My face grew taught, my throat was tight and as I found it hard to swallow I felt a pricking sensation in my eyes. In this moment with Kathy, I was not acting out of inner plans or working things out intellectually or theoretically, rather I was responding to her responses and actions.

Understanding what Kathy was feeling, therefore, did not simply involve her sending me her feelings which she had put into words so that I could

made sense of them intellectually. Rather than a process of sending messages from her body to my mind, understanding her feeling involved
responding to each other's responses. Kathy's responses affected my
body and positioned me to notice what touched me as important for our
making sense together. By constantly checking whether my understanding fitted with her understanding we went on to co-ordinate and generate our joint understanding. In this way we may see the body not as a
container of feelings but as a communicator of feelings that gives us clues
so that we can notice and try to make sense. Generating understanding
therefore involves giving and responding to clues with each other.

Since we live within and through our bodies, communicating feelings to
each other and understanding each other's feelings always involves the body.
Thus language and the spoken word cannot be understood as separate from
the body since the act of speaking involves the ways we gesture to each other
with our bodies through facial expression, tone of voice, gaze of eyes,
breathing, posture and muscle tension. Tom Andersen (1995) wonders what
would happen if we were to think of ourselves as touching each other in
conversation rather than listening and talking and invites us to consider what
words we might use to describe the ways we touch others. For example are
we stroking, pressing, holding, pushing, grabbing, hitting or are we trying
to avoid touching by ignoring, overlooking or pushing away?

The face, in particular, plays a crucial role in both communicating and
understanding each other's feelings. Automatically our gaze goes to the face
of the other and scans the eyes and mouth in detail (Griffith and Elliott Griffith, 1994). Thus we touch and move each other with our facial expressions
and often it is the facial display that directs people's attention to what needs
to be noticed so that those involved can begin to make sense.

> Having just walked onto the paediatric ward, a nurse informed me seven-year-
> old Paul S had died a few hours earlier. His father, I was told, was waiting to
> see me in Paul's cubicle. I had been qualified as a clinical psychologist for only
> a couple of years and Paul and his family were the first family I had worked with
> intensively where a child was dying from a life-threatening illness. His parents
> were always keen to talk when they brought Paul to the hospital so I expected
> his father would want to see me. When I entered the cubicle, however, I was
> surprised to see Paul lying on the bed, and several adult members of their fam-
> ily and community kneeling around him. As Mr S got up to walk towards me,
> the others began to sing and hum. As I walked towards Mr S, my gaze met his
> brimming eyes and I could feel the corners of my mouth pulling down despite
> my best efforts to still it. Mr S offered me his hand and the words, 'Thank you
> for coming.' I felt a tear roll down my cheek.

> When I got the chance to leave the ward that morning, I found myself
> sobbing as I ran the mile and a half down the road to my supervisor's
> office. When I found her I related my experience with Paul's father,

distressed that I had 'acted unprofessionally'. I was questioning whether I should be working with families with very ill children if I was 'not cut out to manage my emotions'. In a quiet and gentle way she related the following story of her own experience:

'I was involved in a seven-car pile-up on the motorway during a heavy storm. A car had hit mine from behind and I had hit my head against the steering-wheel when I went into the car ahead of me. I was staring ahead of me in a daze when a man opened the door of my car. He asked if I was all right. As I looked up I saw absolute shock or horror in his face. I began to cry. It was as if I had seen my own shock and the horror of my experience in his face. Perhaps it was useful for Paul's father to see his distress in your face.'

Resonating in our emotion

Above, my supervisor reflects something of the process of resonating in emotion. The man opening the door of her car displayed an expression on his face, perhaps horror or fear or distress, in response to what he had already seen of the accident. Perhaps, co-ordinating with her bodily actions, he was also adopting something of her facial expression. In turn my supervisor responded to his response, perhaps adopting something of his expression. In this way, they were shaping and reshaping each other's bodily responses.

The results of the research of Paul Ekman and his colleagues (Ekman, Levenson and Friesen, 1983) suggest something of the process whereby resonating in emotion occurs. They asked participants to arrange their facial muscles in certain patterns involved in particular emotions, for example happiness (smile, lips widened and out) or anger (frown, clenched jaw). The instructions were given in a way that the participants could not have known they were being asked to mimic the display of particular emotions. Having been induced to adopt these facial expressions, the participants were then asked how they felt. Although participants did not recognize the purpose or even the nature of the expressions that they were led to adopt, they reported changes in feelings that corresponded to the expressions. For example, when asked to induce facial expressions of happiness, they reported feeling happy, and with expressions of anger they reported feeling angry. Ekman's research has shown that adopting specific facial displays to mimic particular emotions may actually induce people to experience such emotion states. Therefore resonating with each other in emotion involves co-ordinating our bodies, and the facial expressions and postures we adopt affect the feelings we go on to experience. I responded to Paul's father's response with bodily responses and actions of my own and he in turn responded to my responses. As my gaze moved to his eyes and mouth I felt my mouth pull down and my eyes fill. In this way I was co-ordinating with and mirroring some aspects of his expression. In similar ways, mothers mirror or imitate the facial expressions of their children and thereby begin to experience parallel feelings. It is in this way that we are in communication through the 'emotioning' of our bodies.

The display or postures we adopt in co-ordination with others trigger our parallel experience of the affect. We then go on to connect with our previous experiences of that feeling. We bring our own stories and memories of emotional experience that are associated with this feeling from the different contexts of our lives which may help us to appreciate the other's world (Nathanson, 1992).

Listening with our bodies

To the extent that we are willing to mimic or adopt the expression and posture of the other, we can share a parallel version of the feeling they are experiencing. Therefore in therapeutic conversations we can choose to mirror the facial expressions, breathing, posture or bodily movements of clients as a way of 'opening a window into their experience' (Griffith and Elliott Griffith, 1994). Instead of focusing primarily on clients' words or trying to work out what they are meaning cognitively, we can position ourselves to listen with our bodies. Placing ourselves in the bodily configuration of clients, synchronizing our actions with theirs we may then go on to listen from that position.

> Fourteen-year-old Elisabeth G and her parents came to see me at the request of the medical team involved in her care. Elisabeth had multiple medical problems that were not responding to treatment as the doctors expected and they had suggested that a meeting with the team psychologist might help Elisabeth face the challenge of her symptoms.

> When I met Mr G, Elisabeth's father, he refused to shake my hand offered to him in the waiting room. In response to my asking him what name he would prefer me use with him, he informed me in a raised voice that he 'did not ask for this meeting thank you very much' and that he 'could not see the point of coming here'. At the start of our meeting I thought he was going to get up and leave the room. Elisabeth looked at one point crestfallen or perhaps embarrassed by her father's response as she arched her eyebrows and then hung her head towards her lap. At another point she appeared furious or perhaps frightened as she lifted her head, stared fixedly ahead and then frowned, clenching her jaw. Mrs G sat quietly, nodding in agreement with her husband. My inclination was to direct the conversation towards Mrs G and Elisabeth and to avoid eye contact with

Mr G. Aware of my tendency to withdraw from Mr G on the one hand and yet my wish to engage with him rather than lose him to the work with his daughter on the other, I decided to alter my position. Instead of leaning away from him and towards his daughter, as I had begun, therefore, I leaned towards him. I also began to pace my breathing with his so that at first I was taking short breaths and was inhaling more deeply than exhaling. As I synchronized my breathing with his, I began to feel a slight tightness in my chest. The pain in my chest made me wonder what discomfort he might be feeling though I chose not ask this at the time. Experiencing this pain moved me to feel compassion for Mr G. I was able to extend my exhalation and to genuinely thank Mr G for giving up his time to come to the hospital. I also asked with concern, 'You've come all this way – is there anything we can use the time for that would make this journey worth your while?' Mr G also seemed to exhale as he went on to complain that he had had 'no answers from the hospital'. I asked which questions were most pressing for him, his wife and Elisabeth to have answered, and if they would like us to list them so we could think together whom they might approach for the answers.

James Griffith and Melissa Elliott might say that by carefully pacing my breathing and movements with those of Mr G, I could begin to appreciate something of his emotional posture. By synchronizing my breathing with his rapid and shallow breathing and mirroring the stiffness of his posture, I experienced a version of the discomfort he might have been experiencing. Thus I could begin to make some sense of the tightness and loudness of his voice, his avoidance of my gaze and his positioning his body away from the rest of the group. In their beautiful book (Griffith and Elliott Griffith, 1994), they suggest how we might invite people to engage with us in 'emotional postures of tranquility' in which they are relaxed and therefore open to reflecting, wondering, listening and creating with us. In an 'emotional posture of mobilization' people would be vigilant for threat, and therefore physically poised for action, ready to defend or attack, perhaps against anticipated blame, criticism or judgement from us. By slowing the pace of the session and watching and following the bodies of the participants, I was careful to notice whether I was likely to invite postures of tranquility or mobilization.

As our conversation progressed, my attention moved to Mrs G. I noticed that she sat with her shoulders hunched and her body bent forward. As I adjusted my body to adopt her posture I found I could hold it only briefly since I was developing a shooting pain up the back of my neck and at the back of my head. I tentatively asked Mrs G, 'What has this been like for you? Some families in your situation have said that trying to work their way round our medical system has been a constant headache.' Mrs G made a sound something between a laugh and a hiccup and told me, 'I have a splitting headache at this very moment.'

In the examples above, I describe a coupling and co-ordination with people in emotion. I begin by mirroring the postures and following the actions with both Mr and Mrs G. With Mr G I adjust my breathing by extending my exhalation; he responds by slowing and extending his exhalation and in turn I once again synchronize with his breathing. After mirroring Mrs G's posture briefly I have to adjust my position to relieve the discomfort. Mrs G's 'laugh' in response to the word 'headache' seemed to move her to adjust her position, dropping her shoulders and lifting her head.

Melissa Elliott is mindful of not appearing magical or all knowing when she shares her understandings generated through listening with her body. Therefore she takes care to be transparent with clients, reflecting how she is feeling as she listens and then inviting them to consider if there is any connection with their own experience. I adopted this sort of approach with Kathy above when I asked her, 'I am wondering whether what I am feeling and thinking – being here with you – is connected in any way to what you have been going through at all. Would you be interested to hear and tell me if my experience is familiar to you in any way? Maybe it is not.'

Within our cultures we learn which expressions to display in which circumstances (Chapter 3). We also learn how to silence our bodies, including our facial expressions, tone of voice, breathing, posture, and gaze of eyes so as not to communicate our desires or intentions according to our cultural conventions (Ekman, 1972).

> Later on in our work together, Lorna told me that the most distressing symptom of multiple sclerosis for her was that 'sometimes I give it all away'. She went on to explain, 'I have always decided myself what I show people – when I was a child you couldn't read a thing on my face – my mother always said I would never have any lines because I never smiled and I never frowned.'

As Lorna tells me, the desires or intentions we express with our bodies are not always intended for public observation. Therefore Tom Andersen (1991) suggests that we do not comment on, know or understand clients' bodily communications too quickly and rather should take time to establish whether the display was intended for our eyes. Thus it is our challenge to evaluate whether the person's expressions are offerings or invitations or whether they are intending to silence their display because they do not want to communicate.

Connecting the body with emotion stories

Stories hold our emotions together, co-ordinating our bodies with our judgements and actions. In Chapter 3, I suggested how we might bring forth stories connected with emotions by exploring the judgements people make about their feelings. Exploring bodily experiences offers another way into stories of emotion. Therefore, in this chapter I propose an approach to transforming emotion stories that begins with bodily feelings and postures. For example, below I ask Gavin how 'depression' organizes his body.

> Gavin, whom we meet again in Chapter 7, described how 'depression' would come over him 'like a cloud'. When I asked him, 'What does it do to your body, this cloud of depression? Can you feel the depression in your body?' Gavin described a 'pinching' sensation in his shoulders so they were 'tight and sometimes quite sore'. When I asked him to show me what the 'depression' did to his body, he hunched his shoulders towards his ears wincing as he did so. I noticed his shoulders were facing forwards so that his upper back was arched quite considerably, his neck extended forward and his head hung low. Gavin agreed to hold his 'depression' posture a while longer so we might pay attention to what was happening with his body.

Having identified his feelings and bodily posture connected with the emotion, 'depression', I went on to invite Gavin to connect the affects he was experiencing with the story that was co-ordinating his body in this way. That is, I invited him to find the narrative connected to the body posture by asking him about his life experiences connected to these feelings. Hence I asked Gavin to scan his memory for similar or familiar feelings and body postures to the ones he had described.

> *Glenda:* When have you felt this way before in your body? If you turn through the pages of your life, as if it were a book of your life story, what parts of your life are most connected with this body posture? [Griffith and Elliott Griffith, 1994].
>
> Gavin spoke of his loneliness at school. He said that he had always 'felt different' and did not want to 'stick out' or be noticed.

I could have invited Gavin to tell more of his story of 'loneliness at school' with a view to deconstructing the narrative that recruited his body into this emotional posture of loneliness and depression, thus intending to free the posture it was holding in place. I might also have drawn his attention to the ways his story was organizing his body with a view to weakening that connection. Instead of exploring the 'depression' and 'loneliness' stories however, I began with a focus on his body posture connected to these stories. Therefore I invited Gavin to describe his body posture. My intention was to enable Gavin to identify the emotional posture connected with the unwanted feeling, 'depression', and then go on together to find a complementary posture that would preclude the unwanted feeling (Griffith and Elliott Griffith, 1994)

> *Glenda:* Can you tell me what you are doing with your body?

[Gavin seemed completely at a loss for words, and accepted my offer to join him so that we might try to describe his body posture together.]

Glenda: Well for example, your shoulders look very tight, they are quite high up close to your ears. Do they feel that way to you?

Gavin: I think so … [touching his left shoulder and ear with his right hand] Yeah, they do.

Glenda: Do they feel comfortable in that position – your shoulders?

Gavin: No way. [wincing]

Glenda: Can you notice where your neck is … and your head?

Gavin: Here – uh sticking out at the front?

Glenda: Mmmm …. Is that comfortable?

Gavin: No.

Glenda: Is it, does it feel like the pinching tightness you were talking about?

Gavin: It is yeah.

Glenda: And your head? Does it face up or down?

Gavin: Down.

Glenda: So to change that posture of your body to where you feel more comfortable, what would you do?

Gavin: I can let my shoulders down? [Spontaneously breathing out as he drops his shoulders and then rubs the back of his neck, wincing.]

Glenda: What do you notice when you do that? Does it feel better or worse?

Gavin: Better. But I feel more stiff in my neck.

Glenda: Would you like to try out some exercises to release the stiffness from your neck and shoulders? You've sort of worked them out already yourself – now. But we could go over them together now.

Gavin: OK, why not.

For about 20 minutes Gavin and I practised a progressive muscle relaxation technique (Ost, 1987). Focusing on the muscles involved in his unwanted 'depression' posture and his preferred complementary posture, I demonstrated a sequence of tension-release exercises involving the muscle groups of the neck, shoulders and face. By alternating tension and relaxation in these muscles, Gavin was able to discriminate between these two states, distinguish the parts of his body that were playing a central role in the different emotional postures and to learn to shift from his unwanted to his preferred posture. Having invited Gavin to find a new, more comfortable posture, I go on below to invite him to describe what he notices in his body as this new posture develops.

Glenda: Can you describe what you are noticing in your body now as this new feeling is growing?

Gavin: [Nods] Much more relaxed.

Glenda: Where are you feeling more relaxed? Anywhere in particular in your body?

Gavin: My shoulders are – looser.

Glenda: Can you focus on this new feeling, on your body now – is it better than before? Do you prefer this …?

Gavin: Yep

I invited Gavin to recreate his first posture of 'depression' and then to move to the new posture so that he could compare the two, asking, 'Can you show me that body posture again? The way you were doing depression? Now can you change it, move your body so that it feels comfortable, so that the feeling of soreness and depression loosens or lifts a bit? What is the difference between the first posture and what you are feeling now?'

Finding the story connected with the preferred posture

I then go on to invite Gavin to name this preferred posture, the posture that is incompatible with the posture of 'depression' and to connect this preferred posture to a new story. Thus we begin to bring forth the story that co-ordinates his body in the ways that he prefers.

Glenda: Can you give it a name, this new posture, how your body is now? Like you called the last one 'depression'.

Gavin: It's like – what's the opposite of depression?

Glenda: That's a great question. What is your opposite?

Gavin: [laughing] Expression?

Glenda: I like it. Does it fit with how your body feels here? What do you notice in your body as this feeling of uh 'expression' as it grows?

Gavin: No I was joking. I don't really mean expression.

Glenda: Oh. Well this new feeling in your body, the one that is not depression, what do you notice as it grows?

Gavin: I can hold my head up – it feels good.

Glenda: Holding you head up, mmm, so if we start leafing through your life story again. When did you have this feeling, how you are feeling in your body now, of holding your head up?

Gavin lifted his head high and rolled his eyes back, as if he was scanning for a memory of the experience. He related the story of his first job when he was about 18 years old. He was apprenticed as a painter to two 'older men'. At first he was terrified of climbing ladders, convinced he would fall. The older men worked him hard, 'making me do all the dog's work – they never talked to me for the first week ... except they gave orders ... or took the mick.' One day Gavin overheard them talking about him. 'They were saying, "He's all right that new lad. He'll make good. He's a quick learner and he works hard. We struck lucky with this one."' Gavin told me, 'I felt six feet taller that day. No one ever said that about me before.' As Gavin told this story I noticed that his shoulders moved back, releasing his neck which held his head erect. I checked with Gavin, 'When you hold your head high like that – what happens to the pinching feeling ... and to the stiffness in your neck?'

Thus stories co-ordinate the body and the body primes us to recall and tell certain stories and not others. Gavin's first story co-ordinates a shrinking and tightening of his body and this posture of 'depression' in turn invites stories of 'loneliness'. Gavin was able to develop a preferred posture complementary to his unwanted posture of 'depression'. We were then able to work together to situate this preferred posture of 'relaxation' and 'holding head up' within a new and preferred narrative. His second narrative co-ordinates an opening and relaxing of his shoulders and a posture of 'head held high' that opens space for Gavin to go on to speak of his competence. Thus Gavin was able to enact a posture and create feelings that brought forth self-enhancing stories of his abilities and potential rather than self-diminishing stories of incompetence. He was then able to go on to address how he might transport these new preferred bodily practices to the more challenging areas of his life.

In this chapter I introduce the body into our developing story of emotion. Since certain bodily experiences prime us for particular actions, our bodily sensations are inevitably interconnected with our display, how we do or show the feeling. Our judgements are also intricately woven with the ways we 'do' emotion since our judgements inform how we show our feelings and the meanings and values we give to those actions. In Chapter 7, I explore how we might invite people to weave in threads of bodily experience, action and judgement through the multiple contexts of their lives to create a richer and textured emotion thereby transforming the emotion story. Before this, in Chapter 5, I pursue how therapists and counsellors might use supervision and reflection with colleagues to help them transform unhelpful emotional postures.

CHAPTER 5
Preparing emotional postures

In a supervision session, Maureen, a psychologist, noted her 'need to express my irritation with Ellen', her client who had been 'laughing inappropriately' despite 'facing her death, the end' (Chapter 3). As Maureen spoke of her 'irritation' with Ellen, she frowned, her body appeared stiff and I experienced her voice as harsh and booming.

In Chapter 4, I introduced James Griffith and Melissa Elliot Griffith's (1994) notion of 'emotional postures' that involve our body's readiness to respond and focus our attention towards others and ourselves in different ways. In emotional postures of 'tranquillity' our attention is focused towards ourselves as in daydreaming or musing or towards connecting with another person, as in wondering, reflecting, listening or creating. In a relationship marked with tranquillity, therefore, we are able to enjoy the mutual touching of each other with, for example, words, voices, eyes or hands. In emotional postures of 'mobilization', on the other hand, attention is focused outward and our bodies are primed to predict or control the other as in investigating, justifying, scorning, shaming, controlling, distancing, protesting and defending. Touching with words or bodies in a relationship marked by mobilization might be experienced as threatening or entrapping.

The emotional postures we engage in influence the quality of conversation we can have with each other. Postures of tranquillity are more likely to open possibilities for therapeutic dialogue involving mutual listening, reflecting and creating whereas postures of mobilization are more likely to position the other to defend, control, counter-justify or blame. When Maureen stated her need to express her irritation with Ellen, I assumed that she wanted to use her supervision time to help her move from the posture of 'irritation' she had described to a mutual posture of tranquillity, whereby both she and Ellen might engage in listening, reflecting and creating, marked by a mutual curiosity.

Our beliefs, the stories we tell and the discourses that inform them, position us morally, bodily and hence relationally with one another. I had assumed that Maureen's view of Ellen's laughter as 'inappropriate' was informing her posture of 'irritation' with Ellen. I therefore invited Maureen to explore different perspectives on Ellen's 'laughing in the face of death' with the intention that generating together a range of different beliefs and stories about 'laughter and death' might invite Maureen into alternative possible postures with Ellen, for example, curiosity or compassion.

Although Maureen appeared to engage in this exploration with interest, she also complained she was feeling uncomfortable in our conversation.

Maureen: This is making me feel disrespectful – as if I have not been respectful of Ellen. It's not true. I really don't like feeling like this – I respect all my clients … For me it's important to be real. If I can't speak from the gut in supervision without feeling judged, how can I say what I am really feeling?

Deconstructing therapists' emotion discourses

Although I had been working with Maureen for almost a year, we had never reflected transparently on the different emotion discourses informing our respective practices. Despite this we were able to achieve a comfortable co-ordination with a sense of mutual respect in our supervision sessions. In this situation, however, Maureen had found my response somewhat 'precious' (her word) and felt I was judging her negatively. I was grateful Maureen had been able to be so frank with me in this conversation since it gave us the opportunity to share details of the emotion discourses informing our conversations in her supervision sessions.

Glenda: Help me understand a bit more where you are coming from. I hear you saying that it is important for you to speak from the gut. Can you help me understand how that helps?

Maureen: It's like ventilating – you get the feeling out so it doesn't interfere in the next session.

Maureen was coming from an autonomous discourse, believing that if she 'ventilated' her feelings about Ellen she could get rid of them and therefore go on to be with Ellen without irritation.

Glenda: Are you saying that you were seeing the irritation as interfering in your relationship with Ellen?

Maureen: [nodding]

Glenda: So your intention is to express the irritation here so that you can get rid of it so you can move on with Ellen, uninterrupted by irritation, and have a different sort of relationship with Ellen?

Maureen: Yes.

Glenda: That's interesting because I think we have very similar intentions here – to do something with that irritation so that it does not interfere with your relationship with Ellen.

Maureen: I know. I don't want to hold on to the irritation. That's the point.

Glenda: How did it affect how you could be with Ellen – the irritation?

Maureen: I couldn't think. It was more that I couldn't listen to her. I was preoccupied with feeling I wanted to correct her and knowing that I shouldn't and then thinking about colluding and not what she was saying.

Above Maureen describes how 'irritation' positioned her to correct Ellen, interrupting her listening and thinking and thus interfering in her relationship with Ellen. For Maureen this was an unwanted emotion, therefore she brought the irritation to supervision with the intention of getting it out of her.

Glenda: Let me tell you where I was coming from. I have found that simply expressing the feeling rarely gets rid of it. Actually my experience has often been the opposite – I find that when I express the feeling I had in a previous session, I do it with words and with my body, and I find that it often stays with me rather than dissipates. It's like I recreate the feeling and in doing so my body takes on the posture of that feeling. Did you take something of the irritation on with your body as you were expressing it with me?

Maureen: I did get worked up going through it all again.

Glenda: I like that phrase – 'worked up'. Mmm, my body sort of works up to the feeling again when I am expressing it after the event. So expressing unwanted feelings about clients to others, like in supervision, seems to position me to re-experience these unwanted feelings and then I am at risk of taking the feelings back with me or on me into the next session with the client. Just describing the feeling and why I'm feeling this way – well it doesn't usually transform the feeling and sometimes it actually consolidates the feeling or works me up to the feeling again.

So what I was trying to do with you was to invite you to transform the feeling by taking different perspectives on the issue of 'death and laughter' that I saw as connected to irritation. My intention was not to judge but to generate new perspectives, new meanings that could enable you to take different positions – almost position your body differently as say curious rather than irritated.

Maureen: That did work. When I started talking about irritation I did get all worked up and when we started looking at my own ideas about laughing when death is near and whether laughing was useful to Ellen, I became interested, curious and I lost that feeling. It would have helped to know what we were doing though.

Glenda: I agree. And now I am wondering whether I should have checked if you had given me enough of a sense of that irritation and also whether the irritation was in any way helpful in your relationship with Ellen?

Our ways of talking can move others and ourselves to action and can change our perceptions, thus morally positioning us in relation to our situations. My conversation with Maureen may have been mirroring something of her conversation with Ellen. Initially when Maureen expressed her irritation with Ellen to me, her emotional posture positioned me in a posture of mobilization. It is likely that I co-ordinated with her frowning, the increased volume of her voice and her stiff posture with my own bodily readiness to control, defend or protest and that my attention was therefore directed to control or change rather than towards reflecting and creating with Maureen. Therefore, when I invited Maureen to take different perspectives on her beliefs about death and laughing it was with the intention of moving her, and myself, from 'irritation' towards 'curiosity' and our mutual co-creating. Although my intended effects were realized in relation to Maureen's posture of irritation with Ellen, Maureen was left feeling bad about herself in our conversation. Maureen went on to suggest that transparency about my intentions could have prevented her from perceiving me as 'precious' and herself as 'disrespectful'.

Approaching emotional expression as a moral choice

Showing an emotion involves adopting a moral stance and taking up a particular relational position (Riikonen and Smith, 1997). Not attending to people's emotional expressions therefore can imply ignoring their moral and relational stances. When Maureen expressed 'irritation' about Ellen in supervision, we might say she was communicating the moral and relational stance she was taking with Ellen. My failure to attend directly to the irritation left her feeling she was not allowed to 'say what I am really feeling' and that I was ignoring her moral and relational positions.

Later in our conversation, above, I approach Maureen's display of the (irritation) emotion with curiosity asking questions about the meaning of her feeling and the effect of expressing this feeling on her relationship with Ellen. In retrospect I recognize that, instead of moving immediately, as I did, to exploring her moral order in relation to 'death and laughing', I could have begun by exploring the moral positions Maureen took in relation to feeling and showing irritation. That is I could have approached her display of the (irritation) emotion as a moral choice, rather than as a ventilation of feelings. Thus I could have explored Maureen's intentions of showing her feeling (of irritation) to me in supervision and her intention to overcome the irritation in sessions with Ellen. For example, I could have asked questions like, 'Are you experiencing something of the irritation you felt with Ellen in the session? How would you like me to respond to your irritation? Would you want Ellen to notice the irritation? What informs your choice to show the irritation here and not with Ellen?'

Talking about her relationship to irritation opened space for Maureen to become increasingly curious about using her beliefs as a resource with Ellen in future sessions.

Using our beliefs about emotion as a resource

In Chapter 4, I discussed how we can shift our emotional postures by changing the stories or beliefs that inform them. I therefore invited Maureen to consider how she might develop a range of ideas about 'death and laughter' to use with Ellen in their future meetings. We began by exploring her beliefs informed by her personal and professional contexts. She had a theory that 'dying is not a laughing matter', informed by stories from her culture, her religion and her psychology training. She also had a theory that 'death is the end' and believed that it was her responsibility to help Ellen 'get in touch with – facing her death, the end'. From her therapy training she knew how to be with Ellen, in particular that 'pushing' could be 'violent' and that joining Ellen in her laughter would be 'colluding' which, she deemed, was inappropriate professional practice. Maureen explained, 'I don't want to collude that everything is just fine. That she's going to live forever. Then I won't be giving space to talk about her fears of dying. She can't do that with anyone else in her family. She has actually told me she has to put on a brave and happy face for them all because they can't cope.'

I explained that we would be approaching each of Maureen's beliefs or stories as a resource that she might use to guide her conversations with Ellen. That is, we would treat each assumption not as a fact or truth that was right or wrong but as a hypothesis (Cecchin, 1987; Cecchin, Lane and Ray, 1994) on which Ellen too may have her own opinions. Hence we went on to contemplate possible themes or stories (Lang and McAdam, 1995) to connect these hypotheses and we used these themes to generate questions that Maureen might ask Ellen.

> For example, having noted her assumption that 'death is not a laughing matter' and the corollary that Ellen had 'nothing to laugh about', Maureen began first to question her own relationship to 'laughing in the face of death' and then grew curious about the meaning of laughter for Ellen. Hence she went on to ask Ellen, a woman in her late 60s, 'Does it feel good to laugh?' 'How would you like me to be with you in your laughter? Would you like me to laugh with you too – or something else?'

Ellen told Maureen, 'Laugh and the whole world laughs with you. Cry and you cry alone.' This created space for Maureen to check if Ellen ever wanted to cry with people, for example, if she thought she might ever like to cry with Maureen – a different kind of crying that would not be alone. Tearfully Ellen said that she much preferred to laugh, that she felt much better with laughing – but 'life is so hard these days'.

Using her own assumptions that 'death is the end' and that Ellen was 'afraid of dying', not as truths or facts but again as themes to inform her questions, Maureen went on to invite Ellen to help her understand Ellen's feelings about her health and her future. Ellen told her she knew she was dying and that this felt 'like an adventure – quite exciting' which came as a surprise to Maureen. She told me Ellen's words had 'shocked' her so that she found herself experiencing her familiar dilemma – 'am I colluding?'. This time, however, Maureen remembered those ideas about joining Ellen in her laughter and so 'decided to join Ellen in her adventure'. Therefore she asked Ellen questions like, 'Who will be with you on your adventure?' and 'Where will your adventure take you?'

In this way Maureen was able to learn that for Ellen, death was not the end and that Ellen had no fears for herself. However, Ellen spoke with tears about her children. She told Maureen she feared for her youngest daughter and for the family after she was gone. She spoke of how she had played a pivotal role in keeping the family together – 'they call me the switchboard' – and she feared they would 'all fall apart' without her. This created the opportunity for Ellen and Maureen to invite her children to talk about how they could 'keep communication lines open' and whether Ellen needed to train some of her family up as 'switchboard operators'.

Initially Maureen began by 'knowing that death is the end', that Ellen would have a 'fear of death' and that Ellen had 'nothing to laugh about since she was dying'. These perspectives informed how she responded to Ellen, positioning her in a posture of 'irritation' when Ellen laughed in the face of death. Informed by the hypotheses and stories we generated in our supervision conversation, Maureen took different positions on her initial assumptions. Thus she explored her ideas about 'death and laughter' from various perspectives and so was able to move from this posture of irritation to one of curiosity in her conversation with Ellen.

Maureen did not reject her initial assumptions or discard them as useless. Instead she approached them as a resource to explore in the conversation with Ellen. Approaching each assumption not as a fact or as a truth, but as a theme to inform her questions, she was able to shift from a posture of irritation to one of curiosity. Thus she was able to move her attention towards understanding and connecting with Ellen through listening, reflecting and wondering and away from justifying her own position or wanting to change or control Ellen's position. Hence Maureen was able to learn how Ellen wanted her to be with her and how they might approach Ellen's future together. Through the back-and-forth interchange of listening, sharing, checking and thereby reciprocal learning and knowing from each other, Ellen and Maureen participated in co-creating responsive understanding.

Following the above conversation with Maureen, I became increasingly attentive to the ways that we co-ordinate emotional postures with people in therapeutic and supervision conversations. Hence I went on to formalize with my team the approach to 'emotional presupposing' that I describe below.

Emotional presupposing

I had been asked to meet with the N family by a nurse colleague, Linda, who was involved in the ongoing medical care of 14-year-old Josie N who had a six year history of diabetes. Josie's father had died from diabetes-related complications, three weeks prior to our scheduled meeting. The nurse was pleased to attend the meeting with the family and assured me that Josie, her mother and 17-year-old sister, Louise, were keen to attend this session. The nurse felt strongly that the family 'need to talk about the father's death and to acknowledge that Josie has the same illness – they have been skirting round the problem for years'.

I generally work with a team when I meet with families. We always allow time before we meet with a family to prepare ourselves for the session. Usually the team joins me in the room with the family although there are also times when we meet together only to help each other prepare for the session. Recently we have specifically dedicated a part of our pre-session preparation to 'emotional presupposing', which involves the team and therapist anticipating the likely emotional flow within the forthcoming therapeutic conversation. Our intention is to help the interviewing therapists prepare themselves for the session by reflecting on the emotional postures they might expect to meet and might themselves carry into the session. If appropriate, the team may help the therapist transform unwanted postures towards preferred positions deemed more likely to invite an atmosphere of respect, safety and collaboration for the people attending the session. Therefore we consider possible ways the therapists might position themselves to create postures of tranquillity.

As part of our pre-session preparation ritual for the meeting with the N family and the nurse Linda therefore, my team colleagues and I began by presupposing what postures we might expect to meet in the session.

We wondered whether the family still wanted this meeting. Perhaps they were feeling numbed following the death of their father and husband and were coming to satisfy the nurse, Linda. Perhaps they were expecting they would have to talk about Mr N or about diabetes when they did not want to. Or perhaps they wanted to share stories about Mr N's death or about his life. Maybe Josie did not want to come at all, worried that she would be blamed for her recent poor diabetic control. Maybe Josie's mother was relieved to be able to have a chat with other adults about how she was going to take care of her daughters or perhaps she was concerned that we would be critical that Josie had not attended her recent hospital appointments.

The team went on to anticipate the possible postures I might hold in the forthcoming conversation with questions like, 'How do you describe your emotional posture now as you are about to meet these people?' They also helped me consider whether these were preferred postures and to contemplate the postures I might wish to create, by exploring the possible implications of the different postures with questions like, 'How might that posture affect your conversation with the people in the room?', 'How might that posture affect the positions you can or can't take in the session with these people?', 'If you adopted a different posture, what might you do?', 'How could you create opportunities for taking alternative positions?'.

> I reflected that I was curious to meet the N family. From what I had heard about them, I anticipated feeling compassion for them all and wanted to position myself so they felt comfortable and respected in our meeting. Therefore I planned to follow the pace and the agenda they set since I was unsure whether they would want to talk at all and what they would want to talk about. I added that I was more concerned about my emotional posture in relation to the nurse, Linda. I presupposed that Linda might be urging me to press the family to talk about their father in the session. I anticipated that I might therefore adopt a posture of protection towards the family and possibly of control or criticism towards Linda, preventing me from working collaboratively with Linda and the family or at worst positioning the family to feel pulled between allying with either Linda or myself.

> As I spoke I was aware that I was growing increasingly antagonistic towards Linda who, I now had come to believe, had coerced the family to attend this appointment. I recognized that entering the conversation with this emotional posture would interfere with creating a useful collaborative dialogue with this family and Linda who was crucial to Josie's care. I therefore asked my team for their help towards transforming my defensive and protective posture.

In situations like these we often use a version of Tom Andersen's (1987) reflecting team approach (Andersen, 1991; Lax, 1995) whereby members of the team have a conversation with each other in front of the interviewing therapist while the therapist is invited to listen. Team members

keep eye contact with one another and talk about the interviewing therapist and consultees in the third person. Separating 'listening' from 'talking' positions in this way is intended to free the interviewing therapists
to take what they find useful from this conversation without the obligation to agree or account, thereby inviting them to become observers to
their own systems. Mindful that talking about the other can magnify
words and experience for the listener, members of the team always try
to present their ideas tentatively and speculatively using qualifiers like
'perhaps', 'maybe' and 'possibly'. Comments are presented as positive
or logical connotations as opposed to criticisms or negative attributions
(Griffith and Elliot Griffith, 1994). Team members offer multiple perspectives on the therapist's dilemma regarding the unwanted emotion,
moving away from taking an either/or position towards both/and or nei-
ther/nor positions.

In our presupposing sessions we have an understanding that the listening
interviewers can stop the team reflections when they have heard sufficient
or if the conversation is proving unhelpful. Team members usually begin
by reflecting on their understanding of the interviewing therapist's experience of the dilemma and the help they are requesting as my team members do below.

Member A: I have heard Glenda say she feels protective towards Josie, her
mother and her sister.

Member B: Yes, and that she is inclined to protect them from pressure to
talk or discuss their feelings in the session. She seems to be saying she
feels pressured by Linda.

Member A: Yes that connects with what I was going to say. Glenda seems to
be describing herself in a posture of mobilization in relation to Linda. She
doesn't seem comfortable with this. She wants to move to a posture of
tranquillity so that she can work collaboratively with Linda and the family.

Member B: I have been thinking about Linda in all this. How she might
arrive. I am wondering whether she might be concerned about how
Glenda sees her. Maybe she will be feeling that Glenda might be critical of
her. I think she would want Glenda to appreciate the work she has been
doing.

Member A: So maybe she is wanting to impress Glenda.

Member B: Yes. So possibly she wants Glenda to notice how hard she has
worked to help Josie or what a good relationship she has with Josie's
mother ...

Member A: Or how deeply she has been affected by Mr N's death and what
the family will have to cope with ...

The above conversation helped to shift me to a markedly different position
in relation to Linda. I was particularly moved by the team's ideas that Linda

might be anticipating my criticism and that she was probably deeply affected by the family's experience. While remaining curious and compassionate
towards the family, I was able to adopt a similar posture in relation to
Linda, opening space for me to become curious about the support she was
receiving for her work with this family. Was she working on her own with
Josie and her family? Whom did she have available to talk to about Mr N's
death? I was mindful of ensuring that Linda would feel respected and
appreciated by me in the meeting. The team's talk therefore moved me to
a different position, replacing my frustration with concern, thereby transforming my posture of defensive antagonism towards curiosity and generosity. Carrying this posture with me into the conversation with Linda and
the N family, I was able to hear Linda's suggestion that the family 'needs
family therapy' as an expression of her concern about the family and hence
to explore with curiosity the concerns of everyone present.

> Mrs N told us she was well supported by her late husband's extended family
> and their church and that she did not see the need to meet with me and my
> team at that time. She expressed considerable appreciation for the help she
> was receiving from Linda with Josie's diabetes. Josie said she was able to talk
> to her older sister about her worries and that she liked seeing Linda for help
> with her diabetes. After the family had left, I talked with Linda about the
> support she was receiving with her work with this family, sharing my
> team's view that working without team support with Josie at this time
> could be emotionally demanding for any worker. Linda spoke at length
> about her worries about the family. She said she had been 'taking them
> home at night' and appreciated our offer of a consultation to her and her
> senior to discuss support for this work in the future.

Emotional presupposing with a team is intended to help interviewing therapists prepare for co-ordinating emotional postures with people in therapeutic conversations. The task is to consider in which emotional posture
one should approach the other and to extend the interviewers' repertoires
of positions they might adopt in the conversation. The team invites the
interviewing therapists to reflect on the postures they might carry into the
conversation, to anticipate how their own postures might fit with those of
the people they are meeting and the implications for choosing to adopt
one posture or another. Where appropriate, therapists are helped to transform emotional postures deemed unwanted or unhelpful towards postures intended to open space for conversations in which people are most
likely to feel safe and respected. In this chapter I have described changing
emotional postures through using our beliefs as resources, reflecting on
multiple perspectives and shifting emotional postures through deconstructing emotion discourses. Emotional presupposing can also incorporate a range of the other relational practices described throughout this

book such as 'externalizing emotion', 'approaching emotion as an invitation', 'deconstructing emotion words and meanings' and 'weaving stories of emotion' which are reviewed in Chapter 7.

In the next chapter, I approach emotions as forms of action. I emphasize a focus on people in relationship with others and describe attempts to make it possible for everyone involved to collaborate in the transforming of emotions.

CHAPTER 6
Performing emotion

A nursing sister from the orthopaedic ward called for my urgent help with 10-year-old Gregory V, who, she said, was 'beside himself with tears'. Gregory 'was refusing' to have his wounds cleaned and dressed. The nurse asked me to 'do some pain management', emphasizing this was 'an emergency – we have allowed him three days – we have to do it now or it will go septic'. Putting down the phone, I scanned my 'inner library' for what I knew about 'distressed children', 'post-surgery', and 'pain management'. Among several metaphorical volumes, I alighted upon recommendations for a cognitive behavioural technique called distraction (McGrath and Goodman, 1998). I ran into a colleague's office asking, 'Have you got some distraction apparatus – I need to do distraction for a painful medical procedure on the orthopaedic ward.' She gave me a bottle of soap bubbles and a blowpipe with a string.

Before I arrived in Gregory's cubicle I had positioned myself to 'know already' (Riikonen, 1999) how to proceed. I had prepared myself with theories and techniques, a set of 'tools' to approach painful medical procedures with children. However, arriving on the ward out of breath, clutching a bottle of soap bubbles and a blowpipe, I found I was unable to use the 'tools' I had selected for distraction from the child's pain in that moment.

I walked into Gregory's cubicle amidst a great commotion. I could just about see a small boy whimpering on his bed since several nurses surrounded him. My eyes were drawn to his bandaged left leg that had been amputated below his knee. Two nurses were talking to him at once, one cajoling and pleading while the other was clearly stating the dangerous consequences of leaving his leg uncleaned. His mother, standing slightly behind him, was stroking his head while a third nurse was tugging at her arm repeating, 'Come and have a cup of tea – he'll be fine'. A physiotherapist put her head round the door and called out to the boy that he could 'come down to play hand ball as soon as it's all over'. I stood and watched for a moment, looking for a place to put myself. I could hardly see the boy. I was feeling claustrophobic and confused.

I remember my efforts to 'stand back' and to 'think' as I stood among the chaos in Gregory's cubicle. I have a recollection of trying to scan through the library in my head again for further theories and tools to inform me how I could respond. Again I was asking myself, 'What do I know?' in an attempt to decide 'What should I do?' Recourse to 'What do I know?', however, did not help me know how to go on but was beginning to position me as if I was outside of and unaffected by what we were all engaged in. In situations like this in the past, I would probably have welcomed a position outside of or away from the intensity of the situation. Therefore I would probably have stepped back to assess and to think about the situation and most likely would have stepped out and away from the activity to consult to the person or people who had called upon me to help. However, this time I did not leave the scene, but instead stayed with Gregory, with his mother and with the ward staff who were all genuinely concerned and trying to do what they thought was best in that moment. Staying with those directly involved enabled me to join the action with Gregory and with his carers and thereby participate in their experience more directly. By remaining in the situation, I was able to notice how I was affected in the moment. Thus I could use this 'knowing from' Gregory, from his carers, from our relationship and from my own experience to help me know how to be with them so as to open space to go on.

> Reflecting my own experience with Gregory in that moment, I said to him, 'I can't really see you properly' and went on to check with him, 'Would it be OK if I open a bit of space here so we can see each other? Would that be OK?' Sniffing and whimpering Gregory nodded. Therefore I asked one of the nurses if it was possible for us to have two chairs. The nurse who was trying to coax Gregory's mother away, darted out of the cubicle as if relieved, and returned with two folding chairs which I opened out in the centre of the room. The atmosphere seemed to quieten as people moved slightly to make space for the chairs. I sat on one chair and asked Gregory, 'Who do you choose to sit on the other chair to talk with us about what we can do here?' He chose his mother and she sat down on the other chair, facing me. I smiled at Gregory's mother and checked whether she was comfortable. She responded with a smile and the words, 'Fine thanks'. I noticed the nurses moving away from Gregory's bed. Some of them were looking around rather awkwardly as if they were wondering where to put themselves. I checked with Gregory whether he could see us, whether he wanted us to move any nearer or whether he could hear what we said well enough. He told me that he could hear and see. I asked Gregory's mother, 'What kinds of things does Gregory like? Do you think I could ask him?' She suggested I could try so I looked over to Gregory and asked, 'What

sorts of things do you like? I mean like football or TV programmes or games or reading – those sorts of things.' Gregory's mother laughed, 'He's football mad!' Gregory and I had a brief chat about football teams in which I asked his advice about which of my local teams I should support. Gregory had strong opinions on the matter pressing me towards 'Spurs' and warning me off 'Arsenhole'. His mother put her hand to her face and looked away from me and towards her son. I was unsure whether she was trying to mask a smile or cover her embarrassment. Several of the nurses giggled. Gregory grinned. I went on, 'So if we make you captain and you choose some of us for your team – who would you choose to help sort this all out?' Gregory pointed to his mother. When I checked with his mother whether she wanted to be on the team, she replied, 'Of course!'

I asked one of the nurses, 'What jobs will team members need to do if the bandages are changed and the operation cleaned in the best way to suit our captain?' The nurse listed the tasks involved, for example removing the bandages by soaking them with warm water; tearing cotton wool and rolling it into balls; soaking the cotton in saline solution; gently dabbing the wounds to remove the encrusted blood and so forth. I asked Gregory, 'So who would you select for the position of bandage soaker? Where would you place that person? And for the position of cotton ball soaker, and of cotton wool tearer? And what position would you give yourself?' One at a time Gregory selected his team. I suggested that each person take up their positions at Gregory's instruction. I checked whether Gregory wanted us to add other jobs to the list. He asked for someone to scratch his back and selected his mother for that position, substituting a nurse into her previous position as cotton ball soaker. I checked where he wanted his mother to stand. We tried out a few positions until Gregory chose a position behind him at the head of his bed. There were some people present who did not have a place in the team. When I asked whether we should keep them on the side as reserves, Gregory suggested he could sell them or transfer them to other teams.

We all completed the cleaning procedure with occasional directions from 'our captain' and agreed to meet in two days' time 'for another practice'.

Stepping in or stepping back

I present an account of this episode here since it marks a transition in my practice. Previously I would have stepped back in an attempt to try and think, thereby creating a distance between me and the others, that is, I would have stepped back in order to go on. In this episode, however, I step in, I step towards and I step with Gregory and his carers. Thus I am making less of an effort to 'think' in the moment, but rather am more mindful of 'what I am doing', of 'how I am responding'. So I find myself reflecting more on 'What should I do?', 'What am I doing?',

'What am I experiencing?' and 'What effect am I having on the others?' rather than 'What do I know?' or 'What do I believe?'

There appears to be a growing culture among psychology and psychotherapy practitioners to offer consultation to hospital ward staff on the management of problems that bring staff and patients into challenging relationships with each other. I notice that there is an expectation, especially from these consultants, that it is preferable to take the sort of 'standing back', 'stepping out' consulting position on hospital wards. I have found that consulting from the outside, whereby staff describe complex patterns of interaction on the ward to me from a distance, involves us in interesting conversations which often, however, do not translate into useful actions that make a difference. Thus giving advice, instruction or direction through words from a distance is often too abstract and disconnected to influence people's performance and misses the opportunity to make a difference to action in the moment. I chose to participate in the action in that moment with Gregory and his carers.

Creating a context of collaboration

When I first entered his cubicle, Gregory appeared alone and isolated. Despite being surrounded by many people trying to help, he sat whimpering on his bed, tears streaming down his face. Gregory's carers were locating the emotions of distress and fear within him. He was being identified as the problem and nurses were placing responsibility for 'refusing treatment' on 'his fear', 'his distress' and sometimes on his mother. Positioning Gregory as 'the problem' or 'with the problem', the nurses were therefore attempting to separate him from his mother in order to help him manage *his* problem, fear or pain. As his mother tried desperately to console her son, a nurse was trying to draw her away for a cup of tea since his mother's actions were construed as making things worse.

If I had joined this process by working individually with Gregory, for example offering him distraction techniques to manage his pain, I could have isolated him further from his carers thereby further contributing to his sense of alienation. Instead I set out to facilitate a context of collaborative relationships, which would include Gregory and all of us involved in his care. By moving from a focus on Gregory as an individual to a focus on our relationships and our joint activity, I intended to create a context in which we could all participate in more rewarding interaction thereby diminishing Gregory's sense of isolation (Anderson, 1999). Working from an assumption that Gregory could accomplish more within a network of collaborative relationships than alone and that we could accomplish more working *with* him than *on* him, I intended to facilitate our joint activity in a way that we might pool the abilities of everyone involved. Thus I pay attention to the relationships between ward staff, parents and patients as much as I attend to the individual, in this case Gregory. My intention is to create opportunities for all involved to participate in interactions with each other that are different from the familiar yet unhelpful patterns that might even be contributing to the individual's distress.

I therefore began by reorganizing the ward environment, inviting people to move and reposition themselves, in order to create spaces and opportunities for people to connect and collaborate with each other in a different way.

Invitation to a different dance

Aware that the medical discourse of the ward would most likely place me in a hierarchical, expert position, to begin with I accepted the ward staff's invitation to take a position of authority on their challenging situation. However, rather than adopting the position of outside observer, advisor or instructor, I chose to exercise the authority afforded me to position myself as a sort of director, conductor or choreographer who both demonstrates and encourages, also accepting positions as participant, player or performer as we continued. Rather than asserting myself as the expert who knows and positioning the others as incompetent, therefore, I positioned Gregory as the 'knower' who was able to act, choose and direct (Sabat, 2001). Thus I invited him to use his abilities to help us perform in ways that could minimize discomfort and relieve distress.

By attending not only to Gregory, the individual, but equally to the relationships of ward staff and Gregory, Gregory and his mother, ward staff and his mother and so forth, I was able to create opportunities for transforming our relationships. Here I was approaching the participants' patterns of relating as a sort of well-rehearsed dance. However, although I joined the dance I also offered different steps thereby helping participants to step out of their practised sequences that reinforced the problem towards generating new routines and new relationships.

Hence we were able to move from a relationship pattern in which Gregory was isolated or alienated from his carers despite being the centre of concern. In this situation the problem had been located within Gregory, and his mother was perceived as contributing to or propping up the problem. However, the more the nurse tried to pull Gregory's mother towards her and away from Gregory, in an attempt to remove her from the situation, the more his mother seemed to be making efforts to comfort Gregory. In this relationship pattern, I stood outside of this activity. By moving my position to the centre of the action and inviting Gregory to elect someone to join me, I ensured that Gregory could see and hear and thus participate in the action. Positioning Gregory as 'our captain' who organized our relationships invited him to collaborate with us in a construction of ourselves as on his side, working towards the same goal and a construction of himself as commanding, important and respected. Thus our relationships could be transformed, enabling a change in the actions of all participants towards one another.

By joining the activity in his cubicle and inviting Gregory to position all of us in relation to himself, I moved away from focusing on Gregory as an individual towards a focus on our team relationships, that is from 'he' to 'we'. Thus I shifted the focus from an individual problem to a joint achievement (McNamee and Gergen, 1999). By facilitating joint activity in this way, we were able to engage each person in the process of working together towards creating solutions.

Extending performance

> When I arrived for our second 'practice' two days later, I found that Gregory's 'team' had begun without me. His mother was standing behind him, rubbing his back, the ward staff had already taken up their positions and Gregory was calling out directions. I watched from the side as the team completed the medical procedure. A nurse then introduced me to a new play specialist, informing me that Gregory had 'bought her in'. Over the next few weeks, Gregory's wounds continued to heal well. Until he left the ward, there was constant talk among staff about which team members he was transferring and buying. The physiotherapist remained desperate to be selected and I learnt that other boys on the ward were asking to have teams of their own.

What fascinated me was how Gregory's team had continued, in my absence, to develop creatively the process we had started together. I may have started off the process by taking the positions of director and choreographer, thereby engaging everyone involved in a joint activity. Having created the conditions for all to collaborate in the 'performance' (Holzman, 1999), I was then able to invite Gregory to position me as one of his team players, thereby positioning him as the director of our joint activity. Thus, I complemented and extended the ward team's familiar dance including new steps and moves that made new relationships and new actions possible. Gregory, taking over the role of director (captain) with great aplomb, with the help of his ward team, was then able to complete what I had started. In later 'practice' sessions Gregory's team went on to elaborate the performance we had started together while I progressed from positions of director and choreographer, to team player and co-performer and then to spectator, audience and witness to their performances. Gregory and his team's abilities to extend their performance resonates with my personal story below.

> When I was in my early years at school, I spent a lot of time agonizing about whether to use my right or left hand to hold the pencil or

paintbrush. Consequently, I struggled with drawing, painting and writing for some time. I can recall many moments of frustrated disappointment on noticing that my seemingly errant hand or arm had yet again dragged smudges of ink, charcoal or paint across the clean cream page of paper which, until then, had been filled with creative possibilities of the images I was imagining.

One episode, however, marked a change in my relationship to working with pencils and paint. Having laid out paints and paper as usual, our teacher instructed us to mix as many colours as we wished and to paint shapes of different colours to fill the page. I recall enjoying this exercise immensely, being unconstrained by a requirement to create any likeness that would need to be recognized, although as always there were the unwanted smudges and trails evident on the paper.

When I returned to class the next day, I found my school-friends pointing at the classroom walls with great excitement. I joined them to marvel at the 'gallery' of artwork adorning the walls. Each painting showed a brightly coloured object or character edged in black, for example a car, a clown, a boat, a beautiful flower. Among them was a piece bearing my name. It was a dancing lady holding two balls in her hands. I recognized the colours and shapes as my very own as they fitted neatly within the black outline to form this beautiful image. My smudges blended perfectly with her twirling skirt. I was overjoyed with 'my' creation. For many months after that I spent hours painting and drawing (mostly dancing ladies) in my spare time.

This teacher had taken my shapes and colours and given them form. By drawing strong outlines around them, she had pulled a figure from the ground thereby giving structure and meaning to my, until then, formless shapes. In this way she had assisted my performance and this began to speak to me of my abilities. Hence I could say to myself, 'I can do that' which inspired my enthusiasm to continue to engage with these abilities. Thus I could go on to repeat this performance and further to find creative ways of making it my own.

It is this sort of process of 'assisted performance' (Vygotsky, 1978; Newman and Holzman, 1993) that seemed to inspire the enthusiasm of Gregory and his team to engage with their abilities to find more creative solutions. We might say that I enabled Gregory and his carers to pull the figure from the ground. Drawing out their abilities, for example, Gregory's knowledge of football, his mother's commitment and ability to comfort and reassure her son, the nurses' experience with the treatment procedure, I was able to assist them to find a form and structure, Gregory's 'team', that could give meaning to their performances. Initially the team completed and repeated the performance we began together. As the team continued to perform they engaged with their abilities which opened space for them to extend their performance creatively. In this way the nurses were able to go on to form teams with other boys on the ward long after Gregory had left.

A pivotal outcome of our work with Gregory was a transformation of relationships between him and those involved in his care. When I looked in on the second 'practice session' which I have described above, I sensed a very different atmosphere from my first meeting with this group of people. This time there was a lightness and playfulness between them all as they worked together to complete a commonly arduous and often painful medical procedure. It is this sort of playful atmosphere which also seemed to enable Lucy G's carers to perform beyond their usual repertoire of responses to emotions.

Lucy's productive feeling

> Eight-year-old Lucy was on the paediatric ward for chemotherapy treatment of a form of leukaemia that had a good prognosis. She was quiet and 'no problem' on the busy ward but the expression on her face worried nursing and play staff. Lucy had a grimace on her face – her eyes were dull and staring most of the time and her mouth pulled taught, straight across her face so that her cheekbones were raised. No one could make sense of Lucy's face.

> The nurses asked me to 'see' Lucy. When I asked how I might be of help with her, they explained that they wanted me to 'tell us what she is feeling'. So far the staff team could not agree an explanation for Lucy's face. Some people were insisting that she was in pain, sad or angry, while others argued she was fearful and yet others suggested she was trying to be happy.

The nurses were emphasizing the need to name Lucy's feeling before they could go on. However, asking her what she felt had not enabled their relationship with Lucy since either she ignored them or showed more of her face. If they guessed with words like, 'Maybe you're feeling a bit [angry/scared/sad] today', or if they interpreted her response, for example, 'I wonder if you are trying to tell us something', she remained silent. The belief that 'knowing what Lucy feels will help us know what to do' seemed to be constraining the nurses' relationship with the child and creating misunderstanding on the ward. The nurses seemed to be treating Lucy's face as a 'read-out' (Fridlund and Duchaine, 1996) of her inner feelings. Unable to make sense of their 'readings', however, interfered with their ability to engage with her, thus distancing them from her.

> I asked the nurses whether they thought Lucy wanted us to 'read' her face or whether they thought her expression was more of a reflection of her personal experiences or private talks with herself not intended for our comments. I wondered whether they thought her facial expressions were intended to be shown or to be hidden. At first there was a thoughtful silence in response to

my questions. Then one nurse asked, 'But how could we ever know?' I suggested we explore with Lucy whether or not she wanted to talk with us about her feelings and that we consider whether there were other sorts of talking that she might prefer.

To continue dialogue, conversation has to invite the interest of willing participants. So far I had learnt that Lucy did not seem willing or interested in the conversations she was being invited into. I had also learnt that Lucy had a passion for drawing and painting. Therefore I asked her whether she would like to draw how things were going for her.

> Quickly, hardly looking at the paper I had offered her, Lucy drew a shape resembling something like a leaf, or perhaps a mouth with two lips closed. This drawing sparked off more debates and deliberations among the ward team. The nurses took Lucy's drawing, as they had her face, to represent her feeling. For example, some said she was drawing her mouth; others that the lack of care she had taken showed she wanted to be left alone; some suggested she did not know how she felt and others that she was having me on. Their debates and wonderings continued.

Since the nurses were most concerned that they 'could not relate' to Lucy nor connect with her comfortably, I decided to focus on our relationships with Lucy and how we were co-ordinating our actions with each other. Therefore I engaged with her drawing and with her response to me as performances and social forms of action rather than as symbols. That is, I saw Lucy as 'doing' the emotion rather then 'expressing' it and therefore I considered how to follow and join her action and how to respond to her communication rather than how to explain or interpret her expression.

> At our next meeting I asked Lucy if she would like to colour the drawing she had made. She nodded. I asked if she wanted to do it together with me or on her own – if together could she choose me a colour too. I presented Lucy with a set of 25 differently coloured pens. She chose red for herself and handed me an orange pen. I asked for help as to where to colour, whether within the lines or outside. She pointed to a place where I should colour and we worked in silence for some time. After a while I tentatively asked, 'What do you want to call this Lucy?' She shrugged and continued to colour so I coloured with her in silence for a while longer until I asked, 'What do you want to do with it ... this?' Lucy did not respond to me with words. She kept her head down as she continued to colour intently.

To know too quickly by naming too soon or moving too hastily to meaning can sometimes disconnect us from the experience or disengage us from the relationship. Therefore I tried to pace myself by taking my cue from Lucy. I would tentatively offer opportunities to extend our conversation, using

Lucy's responses to guide me. For example, below I put forth the idea to her that we might engage others in our performance. However, her response here suggested to me that this was not the right moment to invite others to join in our activity.

> Tentatively I had asked Lucy, 'Would you like to put this [drawing] here to show everyone – me, Anna [nurse], Patsy [nurse], your mum? If it was here [pointing to the wall] Diane [physiotherapist] could see it and Dr Brian.' Lucy looked up at the wall briefly and then carried on colouring without looking at me or speaking. We continued our joint colouring for about five minutes. When I occasionally checked if I was still working on the correct part, Lucy would nod. At one point I commented, 'I'm not sure if I am doing such a good job here?' and she responded, 'It's good.'

Throughout our interaction, I acknowledged Lucy's competence, always positioning her with the authority to guide our joint action. Thus we continued through a back-and-forth process of my receiving her expressions and actions and responding and checking her responses to my responses.

> After a while I said, 'Or ... you could put it away – we could get you a key – you could lock it up ...' Lucy looked up at me for a moment and then put her head down and continued colouring. I went on, 'You could – uhm – take it out when you want to show it' Still colouring, Lucy responded, 'I could lock it up' and I followed, 'You could. Should I see if we could get you a box to lock it? Who could have the key?' At this point Lucy looked at me with wide eyes and shouted out 'Me!' I checked, 'Only you? Anyone else ... if there's a spare key?' Again she shouted out, ' Me and me – two keys for me.'

Encouraging people to express themselves or communicate their feelings can sometimes, as happened with Lucy and the nurses, disable or obstruct relationships. Instead of asking Lucy to describe her feelings or express what she was feeling, therefore, I had invited her to 'do' or perform her feeling through her preferred medium of drawing. Thus I did not join the nurses in their efforts to interpret Lucy's drawing, thereby looking for the meaning behind or under her drawing. Instead, at our second meeting, I asked her permission to join in with her performance, colouring, always deferring to her authority as to what colour to use, where to colour and so forth.

In an attempt to engage others in our activity, I went on to share the conversation I had had with Lucy about the keys with the ward team, which immediately engaged the play specialists who found a creative way to join the performance.

> The play specialists managed to get Lucy a small metal petty-cash box that they painted and decorated together. Lucy locked her drawing away in the box and kept it in her bedside cabinet together with the three keys. The nurses, play specialist and I began to talk about Lucy's 'feeling'

quite a bit, but only when she unlocked it and let it out of the box. Then we might ask: 'What does it need if we are to care for it?'; 'What food does it like?'; 'How is it getting on today?'; 'What does it want us to do to it/for it/with it?'; 'Could I stroke it? Or not?' At all times Lucy took control over who she chose to see her drawing and who she allowed to join the performance.

I was away from the ward for a few weeks. When I returned I noticed several of the student nurses wearing little pink paper shapes on their lapels. When I asked a student nurse what was happening, she told me, 'Oh, haven't you heard? Lucy's feeling had babies.'

The process is the outcome

Thus we created an environment in which people could perform together and an atmosphere of playful interest involving Lucy and the ward staff with her feeling. A key outcome of our work together with Lucy, as with Gregory, was a change in relationships of those engaged in the process. Instead of instructing staff or consulting to them, I performed with them, assisting them to extend their performances. In both cases, the individual initially identified with the problem (Lucy or Gregory) moved position to join the carers and me in collaboratively creating a therapeutic environment, an environment in which all could perform creatively. In this way, the building of the environment for therapeutic interaction became the therapeutic interaction in and of itself. In this sense it was both the 'tool and the result' of the process (Vygotsky, 1978; Newman and Holzman, 1993). In both cases the presenting problem, Gregory's pain and fear and Lucy's face and feeling, faded into the background as people involved continued to engage in rewarding relationships which generated new meaning.

> A few months after Gregory V had left hospital, a charge nurse on the orthopaedic ward drew my attention to several folding chairs stacked in a corner of the waiting area. He informed me that the consultant paediatrician had been so impressed with our work with Gregory that he had successfully negotiated with management for two folding chairs to be ordered for each cubicle.

We might say that the consultant paediatrician had translated our 'knowing from' Gregory into a 'knowing that' chairs can help with pain management in his attempt to abstract an identifiable technique from the process of our performance. In a similar way the senior play specialist, in her attempt to abstract the key technique accountable for our success with Gregory, complained that 'your team treatment didn't work' after four-year-old Polly had 'refused to choose her team to prepare her for surgery'. The consultant paediatrician and the senior play specialist wanted to 'know already' which techniques to employ in a similar way as I knew, to no avail, to 'use distraction' with Gregory V. However, the risk with 'knowing already' is that it positions us for non-participation as we become more involved in our relationships with received knowledges, averages and categories than with the people seeking our help (Riikonen, 1999).

In this chapter we have approached expressing emotions, whether in the form of spoken or symbolic language, as ways of being with another person rather than as expressions of what is inside. That is we have approached emotions as activities, relationships and performances. Therefore, rather than interpret or extrapolate meanings from people's expressions, we have considered what ways of being together we might create through the use of these expressions (Gergen, 1999). The answer to questions addressing how to be with one another is rarely found in the simple applications of preselected techniques or 'tools' like chair arranging, team selection or cutting out paper feelings. More often we are required to create a 'tool' specific to the presenting situation, to fit with the outcome we wish to generate (Newman and Holzman, 1993). The resulting tool might take any form, for example an emotion name co-created locally (as with Jamie M in Chapter 2), a 'dance' or a 'drawing' and is most likely created in a process of improvization with others in the moment. The creation of the tool is itself a performance and in turn makes possible further creative performances. For example, the local naming of Jamie's feeling opened space for the pleasure we all derived from our joint fashioning of his sculpture. The selection, repositioning and allocation of tasks to Gregory's team invited members' enthusiasm and commitment to team performances as well as the buying, selling and transferring of team members between newly created teams within the ward community. The joint drawing with Lucy generated a playful performance involving all the ward staff in the care of her 'feeling' and the birth of several new feelings. Thus the creation of the tool becomes in and of itself transforming of the relationships of the people participating in the emotion and thereby generating of new activities and new meanings for the emotion.

Although it is not possible to abstract simple techniques and rules from the outcome of our work with Gregory, Lucy and Jamie, there are some pointers we can generate to help us create ways of being together that enable us to transform relationships positively. I present these sorts of guidelines in the conclusion, after reviewing, in Chapter 7, the relational practices that we have considered throughout the book.

Transforming emotion

In Chapter 1, I distinguish autonomous and relational emotion discourses and discuss how they inform how we respond to and work with emotions (see Table 1.1, Chapter 1). In this chapter, I revisit some of the relational practices presented in previous chapters and present further relational practices, connecting them with the discourses that inform them. I summarize the difference between relational and autonomous practices discussed throughout this book towards the end of this chapter in Table 7.1.

Externalizing emotions

According to an autonomous discourse, emotions are an expression of something inside of the individual. Informed by an autonomous perspective therefore, we would locate emotions within the individual's body and approach an emotion as internal to the person (she is full of envy) or belonging to the person who has sole ownership of the emotion (his anger). The feeling is therefore positioned within the person and perceived as a characteristic or trait of the person or indeed as the person per se (he is anxious). Within an autonomous discourse the nurses referred to 'Junior's anger' and Lorna complained that 'they really think I *am* [angry]'. Since emotions are perceived as a personal experience, within this discourse, we would need to clarify ownership of the feeling and encourage each person to acknowledge his or her own feelings. Loyal to an autonomous world view, Grace's manager (Chapter 1) therefore told her, 'you *were* anxious Grace'.

If the emotion is defined as 'a problem' or valued negatively within an autonomous discourse then the person who is or has the (problem) emotion is likely to be defined as *the* problem. Within the process of such internalizing discourses (Epston, 1993) therefore, problem emotion terms are most likely to create negative identities. For example, in Chapters 2 and 3, Lorna and Christine show how a description of their selves as angry created

life-diminishing stories of their identities, and Gary recognizes that acknowledging '*his* unhappiness' leaves him feeling 'less of a man'.

The idea that 'feelings are inside us' is basic to the way of thinking and
relating in most of my personal and professional cultures. Therefore I have
found adopting Michael White's (1989a) approach of externalizing a useful antidote to the allure of engaging in internalizing conversations which
are likely to invite negative stories of identity. Externalizing involves encouraging the people involved to objectify, or at times, personify emotions or
feelings that are experienced as undermining or overwhelming. The feeling is thus positioned outside of the person so that it becomes a separate
entity, thereby separating the person from the (problem) feeling. Externalizing conversations about emotions can thus enable us to avoid creating negative stories of identity when we name the emotions of others, or
indeed of our selves.

In Chapter 1, Denise brought her daughter Anya for help with '*her* fear',
explaining that 'Anya *is* anxious' and locating the fear inside Anya. I invited
Anya and her mother to externalize the fear by exploring the effects of the
fear on all family members and on their relationships.

> *Glenda:* So what does this fear do to you Anya?
>
> *Anya:* It makes me cry.
>
> *Glenda:* So it takes the smile off your face?
>
> *Anya:* [smiling and nodding]
>
> *Glenda:* So does it spoil your fun – or not really?
>
> *Anya:* It does.
>
> *Glenda:* It does? Oh, it really does get in the way of things. Hmm ... how
> does it make things with you and your sister?
>
> *Denise:* Kelly gets fed up because Anya won't go to bed unless she's there.
>
> *Glenda:* So this fear, it's getting in between you and Kelly too?
>
> *Anya:* [Nodding]
>
> *Glenda:* Is it making trouble between you – or don't you mind it so much?
>
> *Anya:* I don't like it – it's big trouble.
>
> *Glenda:* Yes it certainly does sound like trouble. Would you like to think of
> ways of putting it in its place? Some children come here to work out ways
> to shrink fear or trick it. Denise, do you think Anya's dad would be prepared
> to come along to help us work out ways to tackle fear here? ... And what
> about your sister, Anya? Do you think she would come too?

By objectifying the emotion (this fear) and at times personifying it (it's
making trouble between you) I invited the family to talk in a way that
positioned the feeling outside of Anya so that it became a separate entity.
Thus we moved away from seeing the feeling as a trait or characteristic of

Anya or as Anya per se (Anya *is* afraid) and did not attribute the feeling to a property of Anya's sole ownership (Anya *has* anxiety) or as internal to or belonging to Anya (Anya's fear). This enabled a new relationship with the emotion, fear, enhancing personal agency and opening more opportunity for action for Anya and her family. We were therefore able to talk about ways of 'shrinking fear', explore how each family member successfully 'tackled' fear when it 'troubled' them and consider times when we should 'listen to fear' and 'respect fear'.

If we had pursued an internalizing conversation whereby Anya became the emotion (Anya *is* anxious) there would have been little we could do about it other than attempt to change Anya. By being helped to separate her self and her relationships from the emotion through the process of externalization so that the problem was external to her self, Anya could take responsibility for how she interacted with it and was able to involve other family members in this task. The process of externalization therefore opened up the possibility for them to support each other towards tackling fear.

Externalizing anger with Christine, below, (also Chapter 3) included exploring the effects of anger on all aspects of her life including her capacity to enjoy life, her relationships with family and friends, her ability to concentrate on her schoolwork and how she felt about herself.

> Christine was clear that 'anger' was constantly leading her into 'self-hatred' and that it was 'self-hatred' more than 'anger' that was interfering in most areas of her life. Self-hatred was driving a wedge between her and her mother, had completely 'messed up things' with her older sister, was keeping her friends away and was interfering with her studies. Externalizing anger with Christine opened space for us to explore how she had been 'recruited' (White, 1992) into self-hatred and to develop 'antidotes' to counteract 'extreme attacks' of self-loathing. Quite quickly we were able to notice moments of 'self-appreciation'. Once Christine and I had noticed how 'self-appreciation' grew when we gave it a lot of attention, we were able to fend off 'self-hatred' by focusing our work on 'self-appreciation'.

Externalizing anger with Christine created opportunities for her to develop a more positive relationship with herself through identifying and then externalizing self-hatred. I have often noticed that externalizing an unwanted emotion with people can bring other, perhaps unstoried feelings or experiences into the story thereby opening space for co-creating alternative emotion stories.

> For example, when 13-year-old Joanne came for help she said she did 'not want to be sad any more'. When I asked her and her parents what sense they made of this sadness, what theories they had about it, none of them had a clue. When I asked Joanne, 'What effect is this sadness having on

you? How does it make things for you?', she responded tearfully, 'It makes me feel so lonely.' Joanne was able to go on to talk of her isolation in her new school and episodes of bullying of which her parents were unaware.

Externalizing 'sadness' with Joanne, therefore introduced 'loneliness' into the story which created opportunities for us to explore solutions to 'finding company for loneliness' (Joanne's father's idea).

Moving from the intrapersonal to the interactional

Within a relational discourse emotion is viewed as an interpersonal event within a social context in contrast to an autonomous view of emotion as an individual event occurring in isolation within one person's body. A relational perspective therefore views emotion as created between people and hence a social form of action, so that we might approach emotion as a communication or an invitation to others to respond rather than as experienced feelings. Taking an interactional view of emotion therefore positions us more towards finding ways that people can act together rather than feel individually, so that we are more likely to ask, 'What can we do together in this situation?' rather than 'How do you feel?'

In Chapter 1, the nurses had adopted several autonomous practices to deal with Junior A's silence. They named and explained his feeling as 'anger'. They interpreted his silence as grieving for his amputated leg and encouraged expression of his (assumed) feelings of grief and anger. They also educated Junior and his mother about the right ways to feel and respond to his circumstances. Since attributing Junior's silence to anger did not help Mrs A or the nurses find a way to go on with Junior, I invited them to approach Junior's display (of silence) as a communication and an invitation rather than as an expression of 'his anger'. With Junior present I therefore asked them, 'If we look at what Junior is doing at the moment as an invitation from him to us to do something different what might he be inviting us to do or say?' This move positioned all of us to consider the nature of Junior's invitation (What was he asking of us?) and the intention of the communication (What effect did he want his action to have on us?). We were therefore less preoccupied with identifying the correct name for Junior's display, attempting to encourage him to express his anger or analysing his individual feeling. Addressing the intention of Junior's communication and the nature of his invitation opened space for different conversations and actions between Junior, his mother and the ward team, connecting us more with Junior and with each other.

In a supervision session, Anthony, a social worker in a drug rehabilitation unit, discussed his concerns that episodes of violence and aggression were increasing in the unit after each 'feelings group' he was co-facilitating with a nurse colleague. I learnt that Anthony and his co-facilitator saw it as their responsibility to help group participants 'ventilate', 'get in touch with', 'get rid of' or 'deal with' 'their feelings'. They were locating the feelings inside the bodies of each individual group member and commonly would name participants' 'anger' to help them 'own' or 'acknowledge their feelings'.

Adopting the autonomous practices involved in encouraging people to 'express' or 'ventilate' *their* feelings', as Anthony and his colleague were doing above, often has the effect of consolidating or creating the unwanted feelings rather than transforming or creating preferred emotions. When Anthony and his co-facilitator moved away from a focus on naming feelings and facilitating ventilation or expression of emotions and focused instead on addressing the function, consequences and intent of emotions with group participants, they observed a considerable reduction in violent episodes after group sessions.

Anthony and his colleague encouraged participants to talk from their own personal position as well as from the position of other group participants and members of staff. They invited them to approach emotion as an invitation to others to respond (What does this feeling tell me that I want from others? What might Jim be inviting us to do here?) and as a communication with intent (What do I want others to notice/understand by my expression? What effect do I want this action to achieve?). As the group progressed participants were encouraged to attend to the actual effects of their expressions by inviting them to evaluate the efficacy of their communications (Has my action achieved the effect I intended/wanted?). They also invited them to consider how to present their invitations in ways that might more successfully achieve their desired response (How can I invite others to respond to me in the way that I would like?).

Anthony went on to find further creative interactional approaches with this group. For example, he invited participants to locate the emotion they identified within a relationship with questions like, 'This anger you describe, is it between you and Jim here or does it belong more between you and someone else?'; 'What about the disappointment – who is involved in that feeling?'; 'Is this [feeling] between you and your mother or more between you and your social worker?'.

Anthony and his colleague therefore located emotion not in the individual group participants but within relationships, between participants within the group and between participants and staff within the rehabilitation unit. Thus, by moving from intrapersonal practices of naming and analysing feelings to interpersonal practices of locating feelings between people and focusing on intended communication and consequences of actions, they noticed a transformation of relationships including reduced aggression and increased positive interaction within the group and the unit. According to Anthony, encouraging participants to attend to the intended effects of their emotional displays (What effect do I want this action to achieve?) and to note in particular the actual effects of their emotional expressions (Has my action achieved the effect I intended/wanted?) facilitated participants taking more responsibility for their actions.

Anthony and his colleague noted that over time, relationships in the unit as a whole were subtly transformed as people's actions towards one another changed. Group participants became more mindful of the intentions of their communications and the actual effects of their actions. Staff in turn began to use each other more to contemplate what the residents' actions were inviting, for example considering with each other, 'Is his action asking me to engage with him as a parent, a competitor or a supporter?'; 'What effect would accepting this invitation have on his view of himself/our relationships/his relationship with other residents?'. Thus as residents and staff began to talk and respond in different ways so they invited others to treat them differently. Change in relationships in turn created changes for each individual.

Transforming emotion words towards new meanings

Within an autonomous discourse, we are encouraged to think of a set number of core emotions that are innate and universal. The idea is that we can work out what a person is feeling according to his or her facial and bodily expressions. Hence it is considered the responsibility or perhaps even the duty of those in the know to name and explain people's feelings, and experts with appropriate training are deemed well placed to perform this role. Acting out of an autonomous discourse, Grace's manager seemed confident that Grace 'was anxious'. However, we cannot directly access people's subjective bodily experience or private thoughts. Therefore to name what Grace was feeling, her manager would have had to depend on what Grace was showing through her display of the emotion and how her manager was affected by her actions. Noticing the quickening of Grace's breathing and pressure in her speech may have satisfied her manager as sufficient indicators for a description of Grace as 'anxious'. The manager's description however did not fit with Grace's subjective experience.

Our bodily experiences and displays are inevitably involved in emotional episodes since as living beings we continually engage with our surroundings through our bodies. However, the linear correlation of bodily displays with emotional states is not established in that there does not seem to be a set of bodily states that is uniquely and reliably tied to specific emotional states. Also, through our cultures, we learn to involve and experience our bodies in different ways in emotion. In some cultures bodily feelings are taken as the most important aspects of emotion whereas in others, emotions focus solely on public displays without including private bodily feelings at all (Heelas, 1996).

A relational emotion discourse therefore starts from the position that there is no direct correspondence between sensation and meaning. Hence emotions are not perceived as universal and emphasis is placed on how we learn to do emotions as we live in our cultures. Emotions are therefore considered in terms of relationships and meanings rather than classified according to bodily and facial expressions. Since cultures have their own local language and rules, acting out of a relational discourse we would expect a wide range and number of emotions with new emotions emerging and disappearing as cultures evolve. Therefore, in Chapter 2, I propose a relational approach to transforming emotions that moves away from the expert explaining or naming the emotion for the client. Instead I suggest an approach that involves co-creating the name and meaning of the feeling with the client by joining the language of the other, adopting an attitude of curiosity rather than certainty and exploring emotion words through the contexts of people's lives. For example, below, I join Theresa in an exploration of her relationship with 'resentment'.

Transforming resentment

> Theresa phoned asking for an 'urgent' appointment. When she arrived she said she wanted 'help with my resentment'.

I began by joining Theresa in her choice of language. Therefore I used her word, 'resentment', trying to explore her meanings of the word by asking questions. I was interested in Theresa's own meanings of 'resentment' rather than my personal or professional meanings of the word or how it conformed to other 'recognized' theories of emotion. Therefore I asked her, 'Can you help me understand resentment?'

> Theresa told me she had been 'struggling with step four of the 12-steps programme for nearly a year now'. She explained that this was an approach to addiction with which she was engaging through Alcoholics Anonymous and that she had found it particularly helpful. She was trying to make an 'inventory of all my resentments' so that she could move on to 'tell them to another person and a higher power'.

> *Glenda:* Would this mean you could put all these resentments behind you and get on with your life as you would like it to be if you follow this step?
> *Theresa:* [nodding] Sort of ...
> *Glenda:* Does this mean resentment is not a good thing?
> *Theresa:* It's an unnecessary waste of good energies.

Here I was acknowledging Theresa's expertise on this 'resentment'. There-fore instead of adopting an expert position on emotions, on this 'resent-ment' or on Theresa, I adopted a position of curiosity, intending to learn more about 'resentment'. Since the meaning of a word emerges in its use, I invited Theresa to use the word, thereby contextualizing it. I also explored how she evaluated 'resentment', was it desirable or unwanted? I learnt that in the context of the 12-steps programme, for Theresa this 'resentment' recruited her into negative views of her self. When I asked Theresa to explain how resentment wasted or sapped her energies, she began to sit-uate the feeling in the context of her family relationships.

Theresa: It was when I was on holiday in Scotland with my father and the boys. I planned it all. I was so looking forward to it. So he could spend time with his grandchildren and they could be with their Pops without the pressures.

Glenda: Sounds a good plan.

Theresa: It was all so awful. I was full of resentment the whole time. I think they had a good time but I spoiled it all – for myself anyway. I was so resentful and then I'd feel bad and hate myself.

Glenda: Was the resentment pulling you into self-hatred?

Theresa: Yes it was. That's exactly what it was doing. I really didn't want it to be that way.

Glenda: What was happening with resentment? Was there a particular time you could tell me about so I can get a picture …?

Theresa: [sighing] Smoking.

Glenda: Smoking?

Theresa: My father has diabetes and he has not been well. And he was smoking and eating sweets with the children. Buying them rubbish. I was full of resentment. He should be taking care of himself.

Glenda: Was that resentment? Was there anything else there – like were you worrying about your dad's health or were you … uh maybe frightened …? No, you tell me … is there some other feeling in this resentment or is it pure resentment?

Here I caught myself drawn to something of an interpretive analysis whereby I was beginning to name a connection, on Theresa's behalf, between resent-ment and her concerns about her father's health. I checked myself mid-sen-tence, 'No, you tell me …' and went on to explore with her what else was inside Theresa's word 'resentment', 'Is there some other feeling in this resentment or is it pure resentment?' (Andersen, 1995).

Theresa: Yes, uh, probably more worry – he doesn't take care of himself and he has been ill and I couldn't bear it if we lost him.

Glenda: You couldn't bear it if you lost him ... mmm ... Was that the main example of resentment?

Theresa: Not really, I was resentful most of the time.

Glenda: Not all the time? What were the feelings the rest of the time ... like in between the resentment?

Theresa: We had some wonderful moments – we went for a cycle ride and Dad really loved it, and the kids were overjoyed to have him there.

Glenda: On a bike – he was riding too?

Theresa: Yes ... I suppose it is rather amazing isn't it?

Glenda: [nodding] I'd say so. How old is your dad again?

Theresa: Seventy-three.

Glenda: Great. So ... [tentatively] there was joy on this holiday ... not only resentment?

Theresa: But I was so resentful of the way he had no time for the children. He spent the whole time talking about the bungalow. He didn't focus on them. Phoning Patsy and the builders. He should have been focusing on the children but he was more interested in the bungalow.

Glenda: Bungalow – I'm not sure I follow?

Theresa: He's renovating the bungalow, putting down new floors – who cares. Patsy is moving in with him, so of course I understand that he wants to change the house for this new relationship – like making a new start. The builders were there before we left. They smashed mum's dressing table to get it out the door. They smashed it without even trying.

Glenda: [noticing that Theresa gave extra force to the word 'smashed', clenching her jaw and her fist and that she swallowed hard as she said 'mum's dressing table'] Your mum's dressing table? It was in the bungalow?

Theresa: [tearful] They smashed it. It still smelt of her, her perfume and powder the ... the brushes ... [tears rolled down Theresa's cheeks and off her chin. I offered her a box of tissues and we sat for a couple of minutes while she was mopping her eyes and wiping her face]

Theresa: [still crying lightly] I don't expect Dad to suspend his life forever. I'm glad he has someone. I'm pleased for him. It's just the way ... her dressing table ... It was so violent ...

Glenda: [quietly] Theresa, is this resentment? I really don't want to tell you what you are feeling – but you have been very tearful and talking about your mother ... and I was just wondering ... could there be other feelings here as well – or is this pure resentment?

Theresa: I think I'm still grieving for my mum. Could I still be grieving?

Glenda: I remember it's around the time of year of your mum's anniversary, isn't it?

Theresa: I hadn't thought of that at all you know.

Glenda: Well I thought of it because I remember you telling me that spring reminds you of your mum … the smells …

Theresa: [nodding tearfully]

Glenda: You know, we've talked more about your worries about your dad today, your worry of losing him and about your grieving for your mum. Is that OK? I mean, we didn't find so much resentment – or do you think we should look for it?

Theresa: [short laugh] We'll probably find it if we look.

Glenda: Is it that once you've listed all your resentments you can't have any more, that's it once you've done steps four and five? Or is it possible to still have a few resentments from time to time?

Theresa: Oh no, of course you have resentments …

Glenda: I may not be understanding this so if my questions are sounding odd or silly, do tell. But as you said, if we look we could find some. So I'm thinking we could wait and see if some appear – maybe they will, maybe they won't – and if they do then if you like we can look at them, or you could list them. Or we could actively go in search of some resentments – I'm not sure how we'd do that – but …

Theresa: [making a circle with her fingers and peering through it] Torch and magnifying glass?

Glenda: A thought … Well I was thinking maybe you should check it out with your sponsor – what she would think – like if maybe you're ready to move to the next step?

Theresa: This has really helped. I don't think I realized how much I still miss my mum … you get on with things …

Theresa initially located 'resentment' in the context of the 12-steps programme. She then went on to tell a story of 'resentment' which involved her father and her children. Later we explored resentment in the context of her relationship with her sponsor. Rather than trying to find out what Theresa was 'really feeling' I concentrated on what she was showing and saying. Allowing her talk to guide my listening gave me the opportunity to learn about her worries about her father and her grief for her mother. These were unexpected understandings that emerged for both Theresa and me and opened opportunities for Theresa in due course to transform her emotion, 'resentment' towards 'grieving'.

Exploring the meanings of 'resentment' through the different contexts of Theresa's life created opportunities for our sharing and extending meanings together. By joining me in an exploration of the contexts that shaped her relationship with 'resentment', Theresa began to transform her relationship with resentment. At first she was dominated by the self-hatred engendered by this emotion as well as her obligation to list, own and to report her resentments. In the course of our conversation she moved towards a curiosity about other possible meanings of the emotion including 'grief'.

Different emotion descriptions open up different possibilities for how to go on. Unique to our cultures, each emotion word carries with it different rights, duties and responsibilities and therefore invites different relationships with self and others. 'Resentment' obligated Theresa to list, own and to report that negatively valued feeling and distanced her from her family as well as led her into self–hatred. 'Grief' on the other hand gave her the right to care for herself, created opportunities to mourn her mother and appreciate her father and engaged her in sharing stories about her mother with her sons that created opportunities for closeness and humour. Naming her emotion as 'grieving' therefore enabled Theresa to have a more positive relationship with herself and others.

When words are examined closely, their meanings can begin to loosen or deconstruct, creating opportunities for new meanings and hence new words to emerge. We can see this process develop as Theresa and I start to look more closely into 'resentment' together. Exploring emotion words through the contexts of people's lives therefore further invites this sort of deconstruction process. Looking at 'resentment' through the contexts of Theresa's relationships with her sponsor, her father, her sons and then later her mother and her father's new partner, further loosened our perspectives on this resentment, opening space for new meanings and descriptions including 'grief' to emerge.

Since feelings are often experienced as ambiguous or mixed rather than pure, multiple descriptions of emotion are usually possible. Asking questions like, 'Does [depression] turn into other emotions sometimes?' or 'Is there some other feeling in this [resentment]?' or 'When are you more likely to express this [disappointment] as [hurt] instead of [anger]?' can also invite this sort of deconstruction, thereby creating opportunities for new meanings and hence different relationships to emerge, as Nita shows us below.

Guilt filled with love

Towards the end of our session, Nita complained of 'guilt' that was 'overwhelming' her, inviting her into prolonged episodes of self-criticism and 'paralysis' and interfering with her relationship with her mother. She explained that she was becoming more impatient with her elderly mother as she became increasingly frail. Past grudges that her mother 'was self-absorbed – she never put me first' kept 'flooding in so I want to get as far away from her as possible at a time when I should be more compassionate'. I asked Nita, 'Is there some other feeling in this guilt or is it pure guilt?' and she replied immediately, 'Love, but that's the problem, it is so painful.' At our next meeting Nita was keen to update me:

Nita: What you said last time. I knew it anyway. You said there must be something else in that guilt, there must be love there too. I knew that. I probably thought it myself before anyway. But it was like you gave me the key – it opened – it made an opening.

Glenda: An opening? What did it open the way for?

Nita: There is love in there as well. A lot of it. Things have been so much better now.

Glenda: How?

Nita: I was listening to the radio and I heard a programme about my mother's illness. People with her condition were describing just what she has been complaining of – even when the doctors are not accepting that it's anything to do with the medication. I thought – that would be a loving thing to do – phone my mum to tell her what I heard. I would probably have done that anyway. But thinking she wouldn't respond – she wouldn't see it. But you know she did.

Glenda: She did – what did she see – do?

Nita: She said, thank you Nitie, that was very good of you to find that out.

Glenda: She did see you doing that in a loving way.

Nita: Yes

Glenda: She responded to your loving?

Nita: She did. That fills me with sadness. [Sighing] I am so very sad. But the guilt is such a small part.

Glenda: Much smaller that the love or the sadness?

Nita: It is – the love is much bigger.

Glenda: What does that open up for you – in other parts of your life – outside of your relationship with your mother?

Nita: I'm thinking much more about intimacy. I don't have any real intimate relationships.

Thus words move and position us rather than simply give us ideas. For Nita, 'guilt' moved her towards self-criticism and 'paralysis' and to a posture of impatience with her mother that brought forth a tendency to dwell on past grudges. Seeing the 'love' in this 'guilt' on the other hand 'made an opening' for Nita to construct her usual generosity towards her mother as 'a loving thing to do' and to notice her mother's reciprocal appreciation. Looking into 'guilt' with Nita in this way thus began to loosen or deconstruct the usual meanings of guilt for Nita so that new feelings (words) like 'love' and later 'sadness' could emerge. Embracing 'love' in turn opened space for Nita to experience 'sadness' and to begin to contemplate her relationship with 'intimacy'.

Transforming emotion words and meanings therefore includes transforming relationships as the words move us and reposition us, shaping our bodies. Through exploring emotion words in this way we also start the process of bringing forth and loosening the stories that hold the emotion together, thereby opening space for creating and telling new stories of emotion. Thus we move away from interpretative analysis, insight and objectification of the individual. Instead we are involved in creating new emotions, a collaborative rather than isolating activity.

Weaving stories of emotion

Throughout this book I challenge the autonomous view that locates emotion within the body of the individual. Instead I take a relational view of emotions as the stories we weave of our physical sensations, display and judgements. Thus I approach bodily experience, action or display and judgements as threads or strands which, when woven together through the multi-layered contexts of our lives, create the story of our emotion. Our relationships and cultures then are the contexts through which we weave these strands of sensation, action and judgements to create the textured story of emotion. Thus stories hold our emotions together, co-ordinating our bodies with our judgements and actions.

When people ask for help with 'feelings' therefore, I take care to avoid reconstituting or creating unwanted emotions through the autonomous practices of naming and interpreting emotions for them as Anthony and his colleague did above. Instead I join them in weaving an emotion story to make sense of their experiences by threading and intertwining strands of their experience, actions and judgements through the many contexts of their lives. The intention of this relational practice is to invite people to elaborate their accounts of an individual feeling or sensation into textured stories of interaction, thereby transforming the emotion by generating or changing the storyline.

To start the weaving process I often invite people to situate their feeling in a sequence of action (How did the feeling come about? When did it begin? How did it develop?) and in the context of interactions (Who else was involved? How did they respond? If I, or someone else, was with you, what would you want us to notice about this feeling? What would you like us to do with this feeling?). Thus I engage with people in creating a story that comprises Bruner's (1990) key features of a narrative including a sequence of events, actions or states involving actors or characters that are connected by a plot to give meaning to the events.

Informed by our emotion discourses we privilege different threads of emotion in our emotion talk so that, for example, bodily experience may not appear in one person's story at all whereas it might present as the striking feature for another person. In emotion talk with clients, therefore, I pay attention to which threads they are privileging and which strands might be absent from the emotion story. For example, I noticed that Sheena (Chapter 1) was privileging bodily experience in her emotion story despite saying that she was unable to experience the sensation in her body. Sheena complained that she was 'not feeling anything' and was clear that she would know she had a feeling if she were to 'feel sick, tight' in her stomach.

I usually begin with the thread of emotion that the client presents to me. If clients place the body in the foreground, I may ask, 'What exactly do you experience in your body?', 'Where in your body does the feeling sit?', 'How does it affect you in your body?'. Thus I asked Sheena, 'Would you be experiencing these feelings anywhere in particular? Would there be a particular place, say, you'd be feeling them … they'd be coming from …? Or not?' And I asked Gavin (Chapter 4), 'What does it do to your body, this cloud of depression? Can you feel the depression in your body?'

If a particular thread is quite absent from the conversation I might introduce the possibility of that thread with a view to weaving a richer textured emotion. For example, for Sheena, displaying or performing the feeling did not particularly stand out in her story. Therefore I could have woven in the thread of action or display with questions like, 'How could you show this feeling?', 'If you were to do the feeling what would you be doing?' or perhaps, 'If you were to paint it/dance it/sing this feeling what would you create?'. Inviting a person to take different positions by thinking of the feeling from the perspectives of others ('What would your daughter notice if she were to see you doing this feeling?') can help people to attend to the display. For example, when I asked Sheena, 'What would I notice if you were feeling something like sadness or anger?' she told me, 'I show a lot through my body – I get very slouchy when I'm low.'

To further texture their emotion story, I also invite people to intertwine different threads. For example, when Sheena reported that she felt 'numb', I could have invited her to connect the thread of bodily experience with a strand of display using questions like, 'If you were to think of these sensations as your body getting ready to do something, what would that something be?' (Griffith and Elliott Griffith, 1994). Or I could have invited her body to tell the story with something like, 'If [the numb part of] your body could be given a voice, what would it say?' In Chapter 4, I invited Gavin to find a preferred body posture complementary to the unwanted 'pinching' sensation in his shoulders he experienced in connection with a feeling of 'depression'. I then went on to invite Gavin to tell the stories connected with his preferred 'head held high' posture which he might go on to transport into other challenging life situations.

In Chapter 2, I showed how asking someone to distinguish or name a feeling is inevitably inviting a judgement about the feeling. Inviting people to evaluate a feeling ('Is it positive or negative to feel this way?') also brings forth judgements. Listening for words like 'must/must not', 'should/should not', 'can/cannot' as moral indicators of what people believe is obligatory, forbidden, expected and permissible, enables us to pay attention to the judgements people are making. Thus I learnt that Theresa negatively evaluated 'resentment', especially in the context of the 12-steps programme.

By inviting clients to weave in threads of experience, action and judgement through the contexts of their lives, we can weave a richer and more textured emotion thereby changing the story. Thus through changing the storyline about the emotion we can create opportunities to change the experience, the display or the judgement. Questions like, 'How do you know you are feeling what you describe?', 'Who else would give it this name?', 'Where do you get your ideas about this emotion from?', 'How were you taught these ideas?', and 'Who else shares your views?' can bring forth layers of contexts like relationship, culture, family or gender, through which we can weave the different threads of the emotion story. In Chapter 3, I showed how to weave the moral judgements people make about their own emotions and those of others through the contexts of their different cultures to create richer and more textured emotions with questions like, 'How do you do unhappiness in your family?', 'Is it expected that as a man or woman in your culture you would show this emotion in this situation?', 'What is your religious view of this emotion?', 'How would a gay man show sadness?'.

Above we have looked at how to join people in the co-creation of an emotion story to make sense of their experience or their responses by inviting them to weave threads of experience, display and judgement through the many contexts of their lives. In a similar way we can help people loosen a narrative that holds an unwanted emotion in place. Weaving in threads of bodily experience, display and judgement therefore thickens or adds texture to the emotion story. Introducing contexts of relationships and cultures both loosens the narrative as well as creating opportunities for further weaving and texturing of the emotion.

Introducing stories of emotion

You will notice that throughout the weaving approach I describe above, I have been asking questions rather than interpreting, explaining or informing people about how they feel. Asking questions from a position of curiosity fits more with the relational practices I present in this book than does the making of statements from an expert position, which fits more with autonomous practices. By asking questions, I intend to 'bring forth' various strands of the emotion story rather than to 'set forth' theories or explanations of emotions from an expert position. That is I am trying to create opportunities for people to weave their own threads of emotion story together rather than attempting to interpret their feelings, tell them what they are feeling or teach them how to feel. However, when people like Lorna in Chapter 3 or Gavin below, specifically make a point of seeking my opinion, I accept their invitation to contribute ideas towards their developing stories of emotion.

> At our third meeting Gavin (Chapter 4) told me, 'depression is not the problem – now I can see that. All the time this has been anger. But I can't get rid of this anger.' Although Gavin had successfully prevented anger from taking over his life and from getting in the way of his relationships, it still 'bothered' him. He repeatedly asked, 'Why am I always so angry? I want to understand.'

In an attempt to avoid imposing my meanings on Gavin and to affirm both his ability and right to make sense of his experience, I began by inviting him to share his own ideas about anger thereby privileging his expertise. Gavin however explained he had 'no ideas' and he wanted my 'professional opinion on this one'. Therefore I responded to Gavin's request by offering or 'setting forth' various professional theories. In chapter 3 I describe how I introduce theories of emotion to people not as truths but as more or less useful ideas that might contribute to the creation of their preferred stories of emotion. Thus I move away from the notion of a hierarchy of knowledges in which professional perspectives are given higher status than personal knowledges or cultural stories (Fredman, 1997). In the course of our conversation below, I offer Gavin the theory that 'emotions function to direct our attention to important concerns' (Arnold and Gasson, 1954).

> *Glenda:* Well there is a theory that says that feelings, like anger, can be like a bulletin or a burglar alarm even. They tell us to take notice that something is happening that's important to us – and we should pay attention to what needs noticing. So according to this theory, anger could be calling your attention to something important for you. What do you think about that idea? Does it begin to help you with understanding anger?
>
> *Gavin:* I don't know. Now I'm sitting here thinking – so then what's it telling me? What is so important that I must pay attention to? And I can't work that one out.

Having shared an emotion theory, I invite clients to evaluate the theory, to decide whether it suits them with questions like, 'Does that fit for you? Which bits of that theory can you use? Which ideas do you want to keep/put away/get rid of? Do you have other ideas that you would like to add?'. Initially Gavin is unsure how he can use the theory I offer him. I go on to offer him a version of the theories I presented to Lorna in Chapter 3, that emotions are communicative (Oatley and Johnson-Laird, 1996) and function to alter our interactions (Oatley, 1996).

> *Glenda:* Well there is another idea that we use emotions like anger to communicate with people, like maybe if we want them to respond to us or we

want to change some things between us.

Gavin: But who would I be communicating with? I keep my anger really private. Do you know, apart from you, I bet no one would even guess how I feel.

Glenda: You keep it private? If I asked the question, 'Who would you like to get a strong message that might be carried by this anger?' or ...

Gavin: [Laughs] My stepfather – but he's dead. Mad isn't it?

Glenda: Mad?

Gavin: You can't get a message to a dead person.

Glenda: Oh ... uh ... would you like to think a bit more about your stepfather – even if he's dead – the message you may want to give him?

Gavin: [Laughs] 'You ruined my life you dirty sod.' Not that he can hear it. Even if he could he wouldn't listen.

Gavin seems interested in this theory but again unsure how it fits with his experience or connects with 'this anger'. I therefore go on to offer him another alternative, a version of the theories that anger adjusts the terms of our relationships (Averill, 1982) and relates to a 'demeaning offence' against ourselves (Lazarus, 1991).

Glenda: There's another theory that says we use anger to kind of change the balance in a relationship with someone. Like if we are feeling put down or humiliated by someone – we use the anger to sort of correct that so we feel, say, more in control ... or like we have more power. I know your stepfather is dead – but does this have any relevance, this theory about changing things between you and him?

Gavin: He always put me down. But I can't see how getting angry at this is going to change things now – he's dead. I mean it's not as if I can give him a piece of my mind and get the better of him – he can't even hear me – even if he could he wouldn't be bothered enough to listen, would he.

Glenda: We are talking about your stepfather now. Can I check if that's OK, Gavin? You were saying you wanted to understand anger. I am not sure if they are connected for you – anger and your stepfather. Don't let me force that connection.

Gavin: No it's OK – of course I am angry with him. But what can I do about it now? What's the point?

Glenda: You said something about changing things now?

Gavin: [nods]

Glenda: So now I am wondering – are there any of these ideas we've been having about anger that might be useful to you for now and the future?

Gavin: I am still thinking about my stepfather. That's what's getting to me – I think. Maybe that's the alarm bell warning me – don't let him ruin your life man.

In the course of our conversation above I share ideas about anger with Gavin based on 'professional' theories. These include 'emotions function as communications to ourselves and others'; 'emotions signal that something needs attention' and 'anger functions to readjust the terms of relationships'. I present these ideas as offerings and invitations to conversation in response to Gavin's request for my 'professional opinion on this one'. Comparing the versions of these theories that I relate to Gavin with the versions I shared with Lorna in Chapter 3, illustrates how each time I relate a theory it evolves in different ways and is modified in relationship with the audience.

Since the theories appear to invoke Gavin's curiosity, together we explore their relevance or fit with his own experience, for example, 'Do they have a relevance?' and 'How might he use them?'. The theories invite Gavin to wonder with me, 'What is [anger] telling me?', 'What is so important to me that I must pay attention?', 'Who would I be communicating with?'. As I engage with Gavin in his wondering, he begins to suggest the connection between his stepfather and the anger he wants to understand and helps me to understand that he wants to address his present situation rather than focus on past relationships with his stepfather and anger. Gavin's understanding that anger may be a warning, 'Do not let him ruin your life', emerged as an opportunity for us to explore in later sessions what he wanted from his life.

Introducing emotion stories to people is intended to enable them to evolve a new preferred emotion story that represents more than just the sum of the individual theories I have shared with them. With the perception of difference, new contexts can evolve giving new meaning to old ideas (Bateson, 1979). Therefore juxtaposing different ideas from a range of theories can invite the person to make new connections between these different theses so creating opportunities for new stories to emerge.

As the client's emotion narrative emerges in our conversation, we can begin to explore if this is a helpful story, what opportunities it offers or what constraints it imposes. For example, as Sheena and I began to create a story about her feeling 'numb' I learnt that she hated feeling numb since she did not feel alive. Sheena believed that 'numb' was not good for her and connected this evaluation with the story of her husband's 'breakdown'. My intention is to participate in the co-creation of preferred stories with people that have a good enough fit with their lived experience and are meaningful and coherent for themselves and those in significant relationship with them. The intention is to enable them to co-ordinate the story that they tell themselves with the stories they share in other significant relationships, for example with family, community, culture or religion. Therefore with the evolving and unfolding of new narratives, I invite people to address the implications and effects of their

stories for themselves, other people and for relationships. I explore how
new or alternative narratives might affect what they might do ('If you decide
that you will like [this story] best, what are you most likely to do/not do?')
and how they might feel ('What effect does holding [this story] have on
you/your daughter?'). I address the possible effects of the different stories on their views of themselves ('If you choose to think that, how does
it affect how you feel about yourself as a person/a woman/a Christian?')
and on their relationships ('How does [this story] affect things between
you and your parents? If you shared this with the vicar what might she or
he say/do/think?'). In this way I begin to contemplate with people the possibilities a new story might create and hence those opportunities for
lived experience made possible for the future.

> With Christine and her mother, a new story emerged suggesting that
> anger can be useful and justified when 'used sparingly' (her mother's
> words) to communicate or get people to respond when 'simple talk' is
> not being heard. Hence we began to think about what Christine would
> like to communicate to whom and what sorts of talk or actions would
> enable her to be heard. Thus a different story from the 'anger is sinful'
> story emerged in which Christine spoke of the 'unfairness' of her illness
> and the 'cruel' treatment she received from school-friends. Christine
> thought that her priest would agree with the view that 'used sparingly'
> anger was justified 'to get people to notice when they are doing wrong'
> but wanted to 'check him out' to make sure. She said she was 'not
> bothered' to tell her friends about the hurt they had inflicted on her in
> the past but felt she would 'feel allowed to confront them if they go
> wrong again'.

Evaluating emotion stories through the different relationship and cultural contexts in this way continues the weaving process both loosening the
narrative as well as opening space for interweaving new threads towards
adding texture to the continually forming emotion.

Table 7.1 Contrasting relational and autonomous emotion practices

Relational practices	Autonomous practices
Externalizing the emotion • position feeling outside of person • separate person from feeling • objectify or personify emotions that are undermining of identity	**Internalizing the emotion** • position feeling within person • encourage people to acknowledge their own feelings • clarify ownership of feeling
Co-creating name and meaning of feeling • join language • ask questions with curiosity • acknowledge other's expertise	**Constructing emotion on behalf of other** • name feeling for other • explain, inform or interpret with certainty • adopt expert position on other's feeling
Approaching display as invitation • explore intended communication • address function and consequences of emotion	**Approaching display as personal expression** • explore how individuals feel • encourage expression of feeling
Deconstructing words/meaning • examine meanings of words closely • look inside words • explore meanings through contexts	**Interpreting and analysing** • interpret or analyse feelings for others • look for meaning behind words • name and explain feelings for others
Weaving preferred story of emotion • change the emotion storyline • weave strands of experience, judgement, action, through contexts • explore the moral order of the emotion	**Facilitating expression and ventilation** • get the feelings out • help get in touch with feelings • educate the right/wrong way to feel
Body as communicator • invite stories connected with preferred body postures	**Body as container** • facilitate ventilation of feelings
Collaborating in joint activity • explore ways people can perform together • approach expression as a form of action • facilitate connections between all involved and affected by the feeling • pool abilities of all involved	**Focusing on individuals** • explore how individuals feel • approach expression as a form of representation • separate the individual displaying the feeling

Towards response-abilities

In the previous pages I have offered a repertoire of emotion practices presented through stories of my own experiences and those of others whom I have joined in conversation. Although it is not possible to abstract simple techniques and rules from the stories and practices I have shared, there are some pointers we can generate to help transform emotion in ways that enhance people's sense of belonging and self-worth. It may have become apparent that my approach suggests that we do not need particularly extraordinary rational knowledges for this. What we do need to develop though is a repertoire of abilities to respond, that is response-abilities enabling us to use and extend our everyday skills to fit with the contexts of the moment (Riikonen, 1999). Below I offer some guiding themes that have enabled my 'response-abilities' and provided me with 'springboards' from which to improvise (Burkitt, 1999).

Reducing isolation

I am guided by the views that everyone has a right to participate in rewarding interaction, that people often suffer when they are not allowed to participate and that people accomplish more in collaboration than alone (Anderson, 1999). Therefore I generally try to avoid or subvert actions like enforced separation or silencing when they are obstructing the involvement of willing participants. When I first met Gregory V (Chapter 6) for example, he appeared alone and isolated despite being surrounded by many people trying to help. I was struck by the apparent alienation of that little boy whimpering on his bed, tears streaming down his face as the nurses tried to draw his mother away from him, and by his mother's determination to stay by her son. By reorganizing the room space, I worked to ensure that Gregory could see and hear us, that he could have a voice if he chose and that he was connected with his mother and whomever else he chose to the extent that he preferred. By acknowledging everyone else in the room as

120

potential team players, I also took care to avoid silencing or undermining anyone else involved in the process since I perceived all his carers as trying to achieve the best outcome for Gregory. By referring to Gregory as 'our captain' I intended to communicate that we were all working as allies in search for a solution to a common problem rather than positioning Gregory as 'the problem' which the rest of us were trying to sort out. In this way we were all able to connect with each other within a collaborative atmosphere.

Moving from individual to relational

Central to my approach, therefore, is a perception of people as not in isolation but as part of relationships, be they families, teams, organizations or cultures. Thus I propose a shift in focus from the individual to the relationship, from the 'he' or 'she' to the 'we' with the consequent move away from a focus on individual intentions, motives or responsibility (Shotter, 1984). Thus I attended as much to the relationships between Junior A (Chapters 1 and 2), Anya (Chapters 1 and 2), Jamie M (Chapter 2), Gregory and Lucy (Chapter 6), and their carers, families, and ward staff as I did to each of them individually. In this way I was locating the emotion not within the individual but within the relationship, thereby focusing on patterns of relating rather than on problems inside people. Approaching the patterns as a relational dance, I seek to join the dance with a view to offering and inviting more enabling steps to the dance (McNamee and Gergen, 1999). For example, when the nurse's attempts to pull Mrs V away from her son Gregory only invited her determined efforts to hold on to her son, I invited the nurse to step out of her practised sequence and created space for Gregory to position his mother. Reorganizing the environment in this way made it possible for everyone to participate in a collaborative activity.

Acknowledging abilities

Since our interactions can support or diminish experiences such as belonging, enthusiasm and self-worth, I work towards facilitating environments in which participants can engage with, extend and develop the sorts of abilities that can speak positively to them of their identities. Rather than asserting myself as the 'knower' and assigning the client as non-competent, therefore, I position the client as the knower. Thus I gave Jamie and Lucy the authority to manage their interactions with their carers by ensuring, for example, that we all referred continually to their expertise on their feelings' uses and how best to respond to them with questions like, 'What is [feeling] up to today? What would you like us to do for/with it now?' I also invited the carers to join me in referring constantly to Gregory's expertise on his team's membership and positioning. Hence we were able to pool the best abilities of everyone involved, both clients and carers, towards making it possible for all of us to go beyond our separate individual abilities.

Avoiding interpretive analysis

I have been approaching expressions as forms of action rather than forms of representation. Rather than looking for meanings behind or under expressions therefore, I look at how meanings emerge and change in the course of interactions. Hence it is not necessary to ensure that all persons have exactly the same understanding of the utterance or symbol. What is necessary is that they develop abilities to co-ordinate their language and actions with each other in ways that make sense and allow them to go on (Cronen and Lang, 1994). In this way Jamie, his parents and significant nurses and doctors mutually co-ordinated in relation to 'balup-balup' without 'knowing' the representational meaning of the word and Lucy and the ward staff co-ordinated towards the production of many new feelings for everybody without 'knowing' the meaning of her face. A good outcome of this approach then is people's enhanced sense of their ability to create and perform in relationship, rather than their proficiency to express themselves.

Throughout this book I have taken the perspective that no one theory provides a universally 'correct', all encompassing, description and explanation of emotion. Yet you, the reader, will have noticed by now that I have favoured relational practices over autonomous practices towards transforming emotions in therapeutic conversations with others. Thus I have not been proposing an 'anything goes' approach to emotions based on a sort of moral relativism. To the contrary, if we are to let go of the idea that there is a right or wrong approach to emotions and acknowledge instead the wide range of possible emotion stories and practices, then the responsibility falls to each of us to consider which emotion practices to adopt. Thus I am proposing that we would need to consider the possible consequences for everyone involved as we adopt one emotion practice rather than another.

Addressing the consequences, opportunities and constraints of adopting different emotion discourses therefore leads us into ethical considerations about how we treat people within the different forms of discourse. Hence we are led to ask ourselves questions like, 'In what ways does this language or vocabulary enhance or diminish how these people value themselves and each other?', 'If I choose this discourse, how will it inform my relationship with this person?', 'How will it enhance or constrain our being together or their being with each other?', 'How will our actions differ if we use this metaphor or another?'. Considerations of the answers to

these sorts of questions have influenced my adopting the relational practices I describe in this book as I work towards bringing forth enhancing rather
than diminishing stories of identity, positive rather than negative experiences
of relationships and creating collaborative rather than isolating experiences for people.

Profiles cross-referenced

Grace

Chapter 1, Chapter 2
Grace, a white English clinical psychologist with whom I talked in supervision, described how she felt frustrated and misunderstood when her manager insisted, 'You were anxious, Grace.'

Junior A

Chapter 1, Chapter 2, Chapter 7
Nine-year-old Junior A had had his leg amputated below the knee. The paediatric nurses asked me to see him and his mother to help with 'his anger' when he stopped eating and speaking. Junior, a black child born in Britain, lived with his mother who came to Britain from the Carribean two years before Junior was born.

Sheena

Chapter 1, Chapter 2
Sheena, a white British woman in her 40s, came for help because she was worried that she was 'not feeling anything' about her mother's recent deterioration with Parkinson's disease and admission to a nursing home. She was concerned that she might 'break down' like her husband Alan if she did not get in touch with her feelings.

Desmond

Chapter 1, Chapter 3
Desmond, a black African charge nurse, participated in one of my training

workshops where he shared his views that a good nurse, 'Puts your feelings aside and gets on with the job.'

Anya

Chapter 1, Chapter 7
Six-year-old Anya lived with her American mother, Denise, English father, Mike, sister Kelly (age 9) and baby brother Michael. Denise sought help because Anya was afraid of going upstairs on her own.

Lorna

Chapter 2, Chapter 3, Chapter 4
Lorna, who had grown up with her mother and brothers in a 'violent family' in Scotland, had been living with a diagnosis of multiple sclerosis for six years since the age of 32. She was permanently confined to a wheelchair and had lost some of the fine motor use of her hands. Lorna had a 'very low opinion' of anger and was more interested in talking about her experiences of 'discrimination' and 'dignity'.

Jamie M

Chapter 2, Chapter 6
Ten-year-old Jamie M had been diagnosed with leukaemia when he was six. For the past four years, following a bone marrow transplant, he had been well. Shortly after his parents were told that the leukaemia had returned and that medical treatment could offer no more than palliative care, Jamie stopped speaking. Jamie and his father made a sculpture of his feeling.

Ellen

Chapter 3, Chapter 5
I discussed Ellen in supervision with a psychologist, Maureen, who described 'irritation' that Ellen was 'laughing inappropriately'. I learnt that Ellen, a woman in her late 60s, was 'facing her death' which she was approaching as 'an adventure'.

Christine B

Chapter 3, Chapter 7
Fifteen-year-old Christine B had undergone surgery, chemotherapy and
radiotherapy for a brain tumour originally identified when she was nine
years old. Christine described 'hating myself' for 'feeling angry' which
according to her Christian beliefs was a 'sin'.

Anthony

Chapter 3, Chapter 7
I met with Anthony for monthly supervision of his work as a social worker
in a drug rehabilitation unit. Anthony was co-facilitating a group for residents in the unit with a nurse colleague.

Gavin

Chapter 4, Chapter 7
Gavin, a white British man in his early 30s who described himself as
'working class', sought help for what he described as 'depression' which
he could feel in his body as a 'pinching' sensation in his shoulders.

References

Andersen T (1987) The reflecting team: dialogue and meta-dialogue in clinical work. Family Process, 26, 415–428.

Andersen T (ed) (1991) The Reflecting Team: Dialogues and Dialogues about Dialogues. New York: Norton.

Andersen T (1992) Reflections on reflecting with families. In: S McNamee and KJ Gergen (eds) Therapy as Social Construction. London: Sage.

Andersen T (1995) Reflecting processes; acts of informing and forming: You can borrow my eyes, but you must not take them away from me! In: S Friedman (ed) The Reflecting Team in Action. Collaborative Practice in Family Therapy. New York: Guilford.

Anderson H (1997) Conversation, Language, and Possibilities. A Postmodern Approach to Therapy. New York: Basic Books.

Anderson H (1999) Collaborative Learning Communities. In: S McNamee and KJ Gergen (eds) Relational Responsibility. Resources for Sustainable Dialogue. London: Sage.

Anderson H, Goolishian H (1992) The client is the expert: a not-knowing approach to therapy. In: S McNamee and KJ Gergen (eds) Therapy as Social Construction. Newbury Park CA: Sage.

Arnold MB, Gasson JA (1954) Feelings and emotions as dynamic factors in personality integration. In: MB Arnold and JA Gasson (eds) The Human Person. New York: Ronald.

Averill JR (1982) Anger and Aggression. An Essay on Emotion. New York: Springer-Verlag.

Averill JR (1996) An analysis of psychophysiological symbolism and its influence on theories of emotion. In: R Harré and WG Parrott (eds) The Emotions. Social, Cultural and Biological Dimensions. London: Sage.

Baron-Cohen S (2003) The Essential Difference. Men, Women and the Extreme Male Brain. London: Allen Lane, The Penguin Press.

Bateson G (1979) Mind and Nature. London: Wildwood Press.

Boscolo L, Cecchin G, Hoffman L, Penn (1987) Milan Systemic Family Therapy. New York: Basic Books.

Bruner J (1990) Acts of Meaning. Cambridge MA: Harvard University Press.

Burkitt I (1999) Relational moves and generative dances. In: S McNamee and KJ Gergen (eds) Relational Responsibility. Resources for Sustainable Dialogue. London: Sage.

Burr V (1995) An Introduction to Social Constructionism. London: Routledge.

Cecchin G (1987) Hypothesizing, circularity and neutrality revisited: an invitation to curiosity, Family Process, 26, 405–413.

Cecchin G, Lane G, Ray WA (1994) The Cybernetics of Prejudices in the Practice of Psychotherapy. London: Karnac.

Crawford J, Kippax S, Onyx J, Gault U, Benton P (1992) Emotion and Gender. London: Sage.

Cronen VE, Johnson KM, Lannaman JW (1982) Paradoxes, double binds, and reflexive loops: an alternative theoretical perspective, Family Process, 20, 91–112.

Cronen V, Lang P (1994) Language and Action: Wittgenstein and Dewey in the practice of therapy and consultation, Human Systems: The Journal of Systemic Consultation and Management, 5, 5–43.

Cross J (1990) An Interview with Judith Cross. Dulwich Centre Newsletter, 3, 26–33.

Darwin C (1872) The expression of emotions in man and animals. Modern paperback edition. Chicago : University of Chicago Press (1965).

Davies B, Harré R (1990) Positioning: the discursive production of selves, Journal for the Theory of Social Behaviour, 20, 43–64.

Durrant M (1990) Saying 'Boo' to Mr Scary: writing a book provides a solution, Family Therapy Case Studies, 5(19), 39–44.

Ekman P (1972) Universals and cultural differences in facial expressions of emotion. In: J Cole (ed) Nebraska Symposium on Motivation, 1971 (Vol 19, pp 207–83). Lincoln, NE: University of Nebraska Press.

Ekman P (1989) The argument and evidence about universals in facial expressions of emotion. In: H Wagner and A Manstead (eds) Handbook of Social Psychophysiology (pp 143–164). Chichester: Wiley.

Ekman P, Levenson RW, Friesen WV (1983) Autonomic nervous system activity distinguishes among emotions, Science, 211: 1208–10.

Epston D (1993) Internalising discourses versus externalising discourses. In: S Gilligan and R Price (eds) Therapeutic Conversations. New York: WW Norton.

Frankl VE (1963) Man's Search for Meaning. New York: Washington Square Press, Simon and Schuster.

Fredman G (1997) Death Talk: Conversations with Children and Families. London: Karnac.

Freedman J, Combs G (1996) Narrative Therapy. The Social Construction of Preferred Realities. New York: WW Norton.

Freud S (1896) Studies in Hysteria. SE Vol 2. London: Hogarth Press.

Freud S (1900) Interpretation of Dreams. SE Vol 4 and 5. London: Hogarth Press.

Freud S (1926) Inhibitions, Symptoms and Anxiety. SE Volume 20, pp 77–178. London: Hogarth Press.

Fridlund AJ, Duchaine B (1996) 'Facial expressions of emotion' and the delusion of the hermetic self. In: R Harré and WG Parrott (eds) The Emotions. Social, Cultural and Biological Dimensions. London: Sage

Gergen KJ (1999) An Invitation to Social Construction. London: Sage.

Griffith JL, Elliott Griffith M (1994) The Body Speaks. Therapeutic Dialogues for Mind–Body Problems. New York: Basic Books.

Harré R, Parrott WG (eds) (1996) The Emotions. Social, Cultural and Biological Dimensions. London: Sage.

Heelas P (1996) Emotion talk across cultures. In R Harré and WG Parrott (eds) The Emotions. Social, Cultural and Biological Dimensions. London: Sage.

Holzman L (1999) Performing Psychology. A Postmodern Culture of the Mind. New York and London: Routledge.

James W (1890) The Principles of Psychology. New York: Henry Holt.

Klein M (1957) Envy and Gratitude. London: Tavistock.

Lang P (1999) Feelings, Emotions and the Language We Live In. KCC Conference, St Stephens College, Oxford.

Lang P, McAdam E (1995) Stories, giving accounts and systemic descriptions. Perspectives and positions in conversations. Feeding and fanning the winds of creative imagination, Human Systems: The Journal of Systemic Consultation and Management, 6, 71–103.

Lax WD (1995) Offering reflections: some theoretical and practical considerations. In: S Friedman (ed) The Reflecting Team in Action: Collaborative Practice in Family Therapy. New York: Guilford Press.

Lazarus RS (1991) Emotion and Adaptation. New York: Oxford University Press.

Lemma A (2000) Humour on the Couch. London: Whurr.

Lowen A (1975) Bioenergetics. New York: Coward, McCann & Geoghagen.

Lutz C (1985) Cultural patterns and individual differences in the child's emotional meaning system. In: M Lewis and C Saarni (eds) The Socialisation of Emotion. New York: Plenum Press.

Lutz CA (1988) Unnatural Emotions. Chicago and London: University of Chicago Press.

Lutz T (1999) Crying. The Natural and Cultural History of Tears. New York: W.W. Norton.

Lyotard J-F (1979) Just Gaming. Minneapolis: University of Minnesota Press.

Lyotard J-F (1984) The Postmodern Condition: A Report on Knowledge. Minneapolis: University of Minnesota Press.

McGrath PJ, Goodman JE (1998) Pain in childhood. In: P Graham (ed) Cognitive-Behaviour Therapy for Children and Families. Cambridge University Press, Cambridge, UK.

McNamee S, Gergen KJ (eds) (1999) Relational Responsibility. Resources for Sustainable Dialogue. London: Sage.

Meichenbaum DH (1985) Stress Inoculation Training. New York: Pergamon Press.

Messent P (2003) Personal communication.

Nathanson DL (1992) Shame and Pride. Affect, Sex, and Birth of the Self. New York: Norton.

Newman F, Holzman L (1993) Lev Vygotsky. Revolutionary Scientist. London and New York: Routledge.

Novaco RW (1977) Stress inoculation: a cognitive therapy for anger, Journal of Consulting and Clinical Psychology, 45, 600–8.

Oatley K (1996) Emotions: communications to the self and others. In: R Harré and WG Parrott (eds) The Emotions. Social, Cultural and Biological Dimensions. London: Sage.

Oatley K, Johnson-Laird PN (1996) The communicative theory of emotions. In: J Jenkins, K Oatley and NL Stein (eds) (1998) Human Emotions. A Reader. Oxford: Blackwell.

Ost LG (1987) Applied relaxation: description of a coping technique and review of controlled studies, Behaviour Research and Therapy, 25, 397–410.

Pearce WB (1989) Communication and the Human Condition. Carbondale: South Illinois University Press.

Riikonen E (1999) Inspiring dialogues and relational responsibility. In: S McNamee and KJ Gergen (eds) Relational Responsibility. Resources for Sustainable Dialogue. London: Sage.

Riikonen E, Smith GM (1997) Re–imagining Therapy. Living Conversations and Relational Knowing. London: Sage.

Sabat SR (2001) The Experience of Alzheimer's Disease. Life through a Tangled Veil. Oxford: Blackwell.

Shawver L (2001) If Wittgenstein and Lyotard could talk with Jack and Jill: towards postmodern family therapy, Journal of Family Therapy, 23, 3, 232–52.

Shotter J (1984) Social Accountability and Selfhood. Oxford: Blackwell.

Shotter J (1993) Conversational Realities. Constructing Life through Language. London: Sage.

Shotter J, Katz AM (1996) Articulating a practice from within the practice itself: establishing formative dialogues by the use of a 'social poetics'. Concepts and Transformations, 2, 71–95.

Stearns PN, Knapp M (1996) Historical perspectives on grief. In: R Harré and WG Parrott (eds) The Emotions. Social, Cultural and Biological Dimensions. London: Sage.

Tomkins SS (1962) Affect, imagery, consciousness. Vol. 1. The positive affects. New York: Springer.

Tomm K (1988). Interventive interviewing. Part III: Intending to ask lineal, circular, strategic or reflexive questions? Family Process, 27 (1), 1–15.

Vygotsky LS (1978) Mind in Society. The Development of Higher Psychological Processes. Cambridge, MA: Harvard University Press.

White M (1989a) The externalising of the problem and the reauthoring of lives and relationships. Selected Papers. Adelaide: Dulwich Centre Publications.

White M (1989b) Fear busting and monster taming: an approach to the fears of young children. Selected Papers. Adelaide: Dulwich Centre Publications.

White M (1992). Deconstruction and Therapy. In: D Epston and M White Experience, Contradiction, Narrative and Imagination: Selected Papers of David Epston and Michael White 1989–1991. Adelaide: Dulwich Centre Publications.

White M, Epston D (1990) Narrative Means to Therapeutic Ends. New York: Norton.

Wittgenstein L (1953) Philosophical Investigations. Oxford: Blackwell.

Index

ability 121
action, social 103
  co-ordinating 15
  synchronizing 70
admiration 37–8
affects, innate 26
aggression 52, 55
Andersen T 30, 68, 72, 84, 101
Anderson H 7, 33, 91, 120
anger 18, 31–2, 33, 51–3 54–5, 115, 117
  as communication 61–2
  externalization of 102
anxiety 48
Arnold MB 115
assisted performance 94–5
authority 121
autonomous discourse 2, 13, 14, 20
autonomous practice 18, 119
Averill JR 27, 61, 116

Baron-Cohen S 10, 35
Bateson G 9
being with 1, 5
beliefs 5
  as a resource 81–3
belonging 2, 3, 121
bodily communication 70
bodily experience 5, 105
bodily knowledge 67–9
body
  as communicator of feeling 5, 68
  /emotional state correlation 105
  organization of 73–5

breathing 68
  pacing of 71, 22
  synchronization of 71, 72
Bruner J 112

catharsis 48, 49
Cecchini G 7, 32, 81
certainty 32
coercion 4, 19, 22
collaboration 1, 2, 91–2
collusion 81–2
colonization of language/emotion talk 3, 22
communication 17
  anger as 61–2
  bodily 68, 70
  and emotion discourse 17
  meaningful 27
  theories 7
  verbal / non–verbal 28
co-ordination 1, 2
  of actions/meanings 15
core emotions 26, 34, 105
Cronen VE 7, 122
cruelty 55
crying 48–9
  as taboo 52–3, 68–9
cultural logic 3
cultural memory 4
culture 9, 34–5
curiosity 8, 27, 32–3, 114

Darwin C 26, 27, 42
depression 48, 73–6
desire 49

DATE DUE

OCT 1 7 2007		
NOV 1 4 2007		
MAY 0 2 2008		
NOV 1 8 2009		
OCT 2 9 2009		

GAYLORD   PRINTED IN U.S.A.

Printed in the United States
48058LVS00003B/175

9 781861 563996